SOCCER TRAINING

D1313450

SOCCER TRAINING

GAMES, DRILLS AND FITNESS PRACTICES
5th edition

Nick Whitehead and Malcolm Cook
Foreword by Alex Ferguson

A & C BLACK · LONDON

Published by A & C Black (Publishers) Ltd
35 Bedford Row, London WC1R 4JH

5th edition 1997
1st edition 1984
2nd edition 1988, reprinted 1989
3rd edition 1992
4th edition 1994, reprinted 1995

© 1994 Nick Whitehead and Malcolm Cook

ISBN 0 7136 3832 X

A CIP catalogue record for this book
is available from the British Library.

Distributed in the USA by
The Talman Company
131 Spring Street
New York, NY 10012.

Acknowledgements
Cover photographs courtesy of Allsport UK Ltd. Weight training
photographs on pages 103–120 by Nigel Farrow. Photograph on
page 10 courtesy of Karl Marshall. All other photographs courtesy
of Sporting Pictures (UK) Ltd.

Typeset in 10½ on 12pt Frutiger Roman by
ABM Typographics Ltd, Hull.
Printed and bound in Great Britain by
Bell & Bain Limited, Thornliebank, Scotland

CONTENTS

Alex Ferguson is a tracksuit manager who believes in working closely with his players on the training field to achieve success.

FOREWORD

Soccer teams, and young players in particular, will benefit from a coaching programme which develops their tactical and organisational skills as well as ball control and general fitness. To this end, the most effective training practices are those requiring a minimum of equipment and explanation, while encouraging progress and enjoyment by breaking up the squad into small, competitive units.

This manual of simple but functional games, drills and fitness practices will provide a vast repertoire of ideas for every team wanting to improve their training success. Authors Malcolm Cook and Nick Whitehead, with impressive backgrounds in soccer and athletics coaching, have combined their specialist knowledge to construct a broad-ranging practical book which balances a wide variety of routines for perfecting specific soccer techniques and tactical understanding with sections on basic warm-up and fitness exercises.

While many of the practices may be familiar to the experienced coach, there are additional ideas for increasing the level of difficulty as the players become more skilled, as well as interesting material for those seeking to try more innovative methods such as weight training.

This excellent book is to be welcomed, and I warmly recommend it to young and aspiring teams at home and abroad.

Alex Ferguson

Alex Ferguson
Team Manager
Manchester United Football Club

Ron Atkinson uses and believes in many of the drills and games contained in this book. He has built up a solid reputation for producing teams with high levels of technical skill and creativity.

INTRODUCTION

This book is designed to offer systematic coaching and training programmes for soccer based on sound learning principles. It contains fundamental games, drills and practices that can be organised with the minimum of equipment to develop technical skills, tactical understanding, speed, endurance and fitness. All the activities are challenging and interesting, and coach and players alike will be able to measure progress.

The book is divided into two parts. Part 1 contains drills and games which are set out to develop major technical skills, goalkeeping and tactics of the game, and caters for all players. The activities begin from a basic level and gradually increase to a more difficult one, thus extending the players in a systematic fashion. Part 2 provides information and guidance on the major fitness components of speed, strength, mobility and endurance, which are often sadly neglected in soccer training programmes. There is an additional section on warming up and muscle stretching which precedes Part 1 because the value of these activities prior to a practice or an actual competitive match is so frequently underestimated that they tend to be omitted from practice schedules.

The emphasis throughout is on purposeful, enjoyable and progressive activities that add variety to the routine of regular soccer training which can be a drudge and also unprofitable if players are provided with the same activities at each practice session. This book will ensure that the soccer coach has a wide repertoire of games, drills and practices at his finger-tips to improve his players' technical skills, tactics and fitness.

Note Throughout the book soccer players and coaches are referred to individually as 'he'. This should, of course, be taken to mean 'he or she' where appropriate.

Alex Ferguson with Malcolm Cook.

WARM-UP AND STRETCHING

Soccer players, like many other sportspeople, are anxious to 'get on with the game'. Unless they can be in the middle of soccer action soon after getting changed, they doubt the value of what they are doing. For many, the time available for training is too short, so they often regard warm-up, mobility, or stretching exercises and skill practices as 'frills'. Even before the start of top-class club or international matches, players fill in the time by just kicking a ball from one to another, hardly ever practising the vigorous sprint runs, or deep lunges, jumps and stretches that will shortly be part of the game.

Research has shown that the warmed-up, stretched body is faster, jumps higher, can kick a ball further, and is less likely to be injured than the unprepared body. Coaches and trainers, therefore, should not only be convinced themselves of the value of warm-up and stretching exercises before training sessions *and* games, but they should also ensure that the players realise the importance of these practices. A knowledge of the fundamentals of warm-up and stretching is necessary so that coaches will know how to convince their players of their value.

Warming up

Before any bouts of vigorous sporting activity, it is usual to prepare the muscles by gentle exercise. The reasons for this are justified differently by various coaches and sportspeople, but seem generally to come under three main headings.

⚽ Those who consider that warming up is an injury-prevention measure point out that when a muscle, or group of muscles, around a joint (the protagonist) contracts, the opposing muscle, or group of muscles, on the other side of the joint (the antagonist) needs to lengthen. Often injuries occur in the 'antagonists' because they have not lengthened sufficiently to allow the vigorous contracting of the 'protagonist' muscles. An obvious example of this is the injury to 'hamstring' muscles at the back of the thigh – the type of injury incurred during vigorous lift of the leg during sprinting. For this reason, some coaches would say that the muscles about to be used should be gradually put through the movements until a full-out effort can be made without risk of injury.

There are, of course, researchers who have shown that when observing sportspeople training without warm-up over a period of time, no injuries were incurred. But to assume that this indicates that warm-up is unnecessary would be an error of judgement, because a variety of factors have to be taken into account, not the least being climate. In very cold weather it could be folly to indulge in explosive muscular activity without gentle jogging and stretching beforehand.

⚽ Those who are of the opinion that warming up is an aid to improving performance illustrate their belief by comparing the body with a motor car. They observe that one would not go into a garage early in the morning and expect a cold car to be driven away at 100 mph. Similarly, they would claim the body needs a short time of adjustment before it becomes most efficient. Some researchers have suggested that the body is most efficient when the pulse rate is between 120 and 180 beats per minute, and that preparatory work is required to bring the body up to 120 beats.

⚽ Many coaches and sportspeople regard the warm-up as psychological preparation for the competition or game ahead. It presents an opportunity for the individual to concentrate his thoughts on the task ahead, mentally rehearse the routines that he is about to perform and, at world-class level, to induce a form of self-hypnosis so that he is oblivious to all that is going on around him which might interfere with or distract him from performing at his best.

Finally, it should be said that whatever the reasons may be, the most successful sportspeople always warm-up before their training *and* competitions, and it seems a wise precaution that anyone involved in physical activity does the same.

Muscle 'stretching'

In addition to its importance in the warm-up, muscle 'stretching' has other advantages. It:

⚽ increases the range of movement through which a limb can act

⚽ promotes good circulation

⚽ prevents muscle injuries.

Stretching should *not* be a vigorous activity, it should be slow and controlled; a feeling of tension as opposed to jerking should be the aim.

During 'stretching' there is a protective mechanism operating called the *stretch reflex*. This is created by a situation in which a nerve signal is passed to the muscles requiring them to *contract*. The muscles being 'stretched'

David Platt and Paul Gascoigne. The coach must have a number of small group activities at his finger-tips which can be used for warm-ups, to improve fitness or to aid team harmony.

actually tighten, which ensures that during the holding of a stretch, or a bouncing movement, the muscles are prevented from tearing. It can therefore be assumed that *muscle fibres* do not 'stretch' but can be lengthened to their normal or 'habit' length during 'stretching' exercises. It is the tissue connecting the fibres, the tendons, the ligaments, the joint capsules *and* the muscles together which must be exercised to ensure improved mobility.

It is also worth noting that muscles are in use on either side of a bone during movement. In the bending of the lower arm towards the shoulder (flexion), the biceps muscles contract (shorten) and on the other side of the upper arm bone (the humerus) the triceps muscles relax. This is called *reciprocal innervation*, meaning that the *protagonist muscles*, the biceps, initiate the movement and a signal goes to the opposing muscles on the other side, the triceps (the *antagonist muscles*), to relax.

Conclusion

⚽ Warm-up, mobility and stretching are subjects which need a knowledge of elementary anatomy and physiology. They are important because not only do they prepare persons for the activity in which they are about to engage, but they also serve long-term purposes of increasing the effectiveness of the individual in a vast number of different movements involved in sport.

⚽ It is important that the warm-up and stretching are not boring. Though each session should start with a jog of up to 1500 metres, depending on the climate, the actual exercises can be changed daily so that the variety is mentally stimulating.

It is not intended to provide detailed information here about warm-up, which, after all, should be at the coach's finger-tips. Many athletics, gymnastics and fitness texts contain exercises from which coaches may select those activities appropriate to their players.

SECTION 1

Coaching, Technical Skills, Tactical Play and Goalkeeping

David Beckham has displayed a cool head under pressure, excellent technical skills and superb match awareness - all the attributes of a future star player.

To obtain maximum benefit from a practice session the coach should pay attention to three organisational elements.

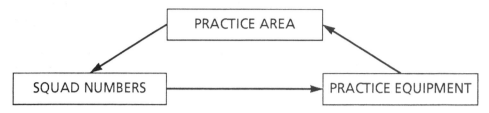

Practice area

Space must be utilised properly and practice areas designated for the squad if the game is to have full effect. Basically, the coach has two 'types' of practice area from which to choose.

(1) Grids   These are a series of squares marked on the ground, measuring 10 x 10 yds, and usually set out on surrounding grass areas to the playing pitch. The grids are flexible and can accommodate large numbers of players working together to improve their technical skills or tactical play by joining or splitting up the squares. For example, in the diagram below, area A measures 20 x 20 yds, area B measures 30 x 20 yds, area C measures 40 x 20 yds, and the total working area measures 60 x 40 yds.

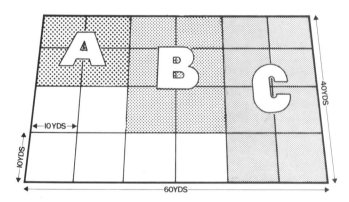

(2) Playing pitch   It is often not possible, or even necessary, to have grids marked on the playing pitch, since its own markings, with varying dimensions and shapes, can be utilised most effectively. In general, the game should take place in the *direction* and *area* where the players mainly operate in their respective functions during the actual game. However, this is not always possible due to the changing state of the playing pitch and particularly muddy goal mouths. Whatever area selected, the coach must ensure that the dimensions are realistic for the number of players at his disposal, otherwise the game will lose much of its effectiveness. As a rule of thumb the following guide-lines apply: games to develop dribbling, screening and tackling should have 'tighter' areas; games for shooting should have a shorter and narrower pitch to encourage shots; crossing and heading practices require a shorter, but wider, area for crosses to be delivered well. Passing and control are best performed in a medium size area; long passing requires a longish and narrow area. As improvements are made, the general dimensions can be reduced so that the players learn to perform their technical skills and tactics in tighter circumstances – just like the 'real' game.

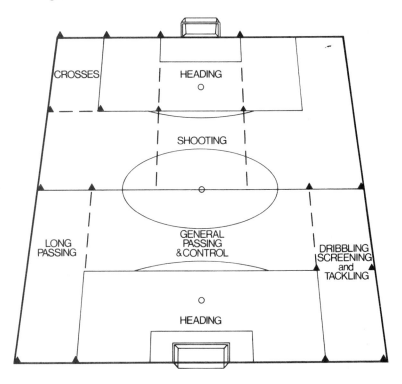

Coaching

The games and drills described in the following chapters can be used by the coach for his squad of between 12 and 22 players. The games, which are designed to develop individual technical skills and group or team tactical play, are used by top coaches from all over the world in various forms to improve their teams and players. Some of the games are 'old-time favourites', while others are more recent; however, they have all been tried and tested and can be recommended to the soccer coach for use with his squad during practice sessions. All are set out logically, showing the purpose, organisational requirements, procedure, scoring and development. The advantages of these games are as follows.

Continuity
The games have little or no stoppages, and plenty of action with everyone involved in continuous play where they can learn skills or tactics.

Simplicity
The games are easy to organise, with simple procedures for scoring and setting up. The coach can leave players unsupervised to some extent and know that their interest will be maintained and learning will still take place even though he is not always directly present at the practice.

Coaching
The design of the games means that players get maximum repetition of certain technical skills and tactical play, thus cutting down the need for long verbal descriptions or demonstrations from the coach. The key coaching factors can be given by the coach beforehand, leaving the players with more practice time in which to perfect their performances.

Progression
The coach can make the games more or less difficult to suit the ability/range of the players in his squad by:

⚽ adding or subtracting players so that one group, having an added numerical advantage, 'outweighs' another, thus giving them success by either making their task easier or more difficult as they start to improve

⚽ reducing or enlarging the practice area to put more or less pressure on technical skills or tactical play by giving players more or less space and time in which to perform

⚽ introducing new rules or 'conditions' for certain individuals, or all players involved in the game, to stress a particular technical skill or tactic. The condition can either make things a little easier or more difficult for the player. For example, some players could play 'free', with as many touches of the ball as required, while others would only play 'one-touch' as their condition.

As a rule, the coach should look to give players early success with new skills or tactics, and should then gradually progress by making success more difficult to attain by increasing pressure on the players' and squad's technical skills and tactics.

Competition

The games have a 'built in' competitive scoring element which can be used by the coach to improve the players' performances if he introduces group team competitions. Each player's performance within a given time limit is totalled up and added to the group team score for comparison. This will help to maintain the motivational level of the players and also to reproduce their technical skills and tactical play in the actual competitive game more effectively.

To get the best out of the games, the coach should consider the following.

(1) Conditions
The 'conditions' to any game or rules, the punishments for infringements and awards for goals, etc., must be communicated clearly to all players involved in the game so that there are no misunderstandings.

(2) Supervision
When the coach is not available to supervise a game, try to delegate a player who is acting as retriever to be referee, with power to award free-kicks and deduct points, and generally see that the rules of the game are followed. A player with authority will best be able to handle the situation, e.g. the team captain or another senior player.

(3) Patience
The players and the coach will need patience when learning to play a new game, since errors will be made until they become familiar with the rules and general demands of the game. The coach must see that the players do not give in too soon, and must show patience and perseverance at all times, especially with skills and tactics they find particularly difficult.

Finally, the coach should remember that these games are not an excuse for him to neglect his coaching duties; the value of the games is in their easy organisation and design, which will give him many opportunities to teach specific technical skill or tactical objectives to some depth.

Squad numbers

The coach will need to deal with varying numbers in his squad, depending on players' availability. The coach can add to, subtract from or generally manipulate his squad to emphasise attacking or defensive aspects of play. Players who are surplus to immediate requirements should still be fruitfully involved in the game by acting as servers or retrievers of the ball. To provide better organisation and motivation for players, it is best to have several small group 'teams' within the squad, each with a definite role to fulfil for a set period of time before 'rotating' to change roles with another group team. In this way, the coach can keep all the players involved in a competitive game.

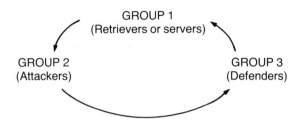

GROUP 1
(Retrievers or servers)

GROUP 2
(Attackers)

GROUP 3
(Defenders)

Practice equipment

Safe and easy, portable equipment is important for marking out the practice areas for the squad. Coloured traffic cones are lightweight and not only give good visual impact and clear identification of the games areas, but they can also be used quickly to alter the sizes of an area. Corner posts with sharp points can be driven through holes in the centre of the cones and into the ground to make a more stable goal. Where stated in a game, full sized goals, either portable or static, should be used with nets for realism. Where this is not possible, due to cost, etc., the goals, each 8yds wide, should be made up with posts and cones as described. Coloured training bibs or shirts will help with identification and make the game more enjoyable. The number of balls at a coach's disposal is important as some games can only be played with a certain number. The quality and weight of the balls are important as well; if they are too heavy, too light or distorted in shape they can spoil the continuity of a game. For example, heavy balls may prove painful for players during heading games.

A CONTROL AND PASSING

SHUTTLE DRILL

Purpose

To develop short/medium/long-range passing techniques and ground/aerial control.

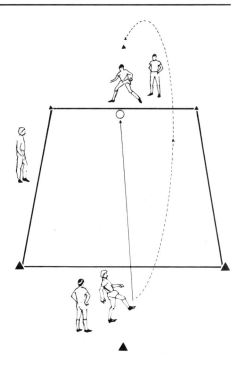

Procedure

The squad splits into smaller groups on an area 20 x 20 yds (longer for long passing). Players line up in two files facing each other, with the first player on one side with a ball at his feet. He proceeds to pass it directly across to the first player on the other side, following in the same direction to join the back of the line and await his next turn. The player receiving the ball controls it and passes it back across to the next player on the opposite side; he also follows the ball to join up at the rear of the line, and so the sequence continues. Each player must not run directly in the same line as his pass, otherwise he will block the next pass; he should run wide outside the line of the ball.

Development

⚽ Condition play to 'two-touch' and then 'one-touch' soccer and record which group achieves the most accurate passes in a given time period.

⚽ The area may be widened or lengthened; players can perform other techniques, such as instep pass, chipped pass, chest control or bended pass.

ONE-TWO PASSING DRILL

Purpose

To develop wall-passing techniques.

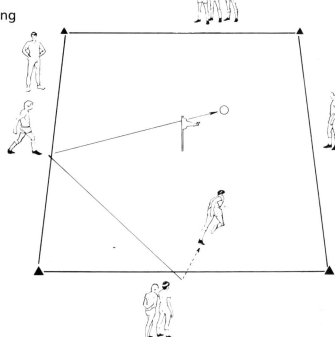

Procedure

A number of players arrange themselves in two files and stand diagonally opposite each other in an area approximately 30 x 20yds wide. A post is placed at the centre of the area. The leading player from one file plays a firm pass to the feet of the next player on the opposite side who comes at a wide angle to meet the ball. The latter then relays it first-time behind the post so that it coincides with the passer who should have run forwards to receive the ball and complete the one-two passing move. Both players carry on to their respective sides and the next two players from each file proceed to play a wall-pass from the opposite direction, and thus the sequence continues.

Development

⚽ Count the number of successful wall-passes in a given time period.

⚽ Instead of a post, use an active player who must stay and defend the central zone while the players from both sides try to play wall-passes past him. The wall-pass, in this case, can be played to either side of the defender.

TRIANGLE DRILL

Purpose

To develop basic reverse passing and controlling techniques.

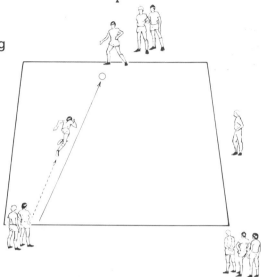

Procedure

The squad splits up into three groups and each group stands at a cone; only one player has a ball at his feet. These cones are approximately 20–50yds away from each other in a wide-angled triangle. There are also three markers to form a bigger triangle a further 15–20yds away; one player from each group should stand at a flag with a ball at his feet. On the signal, the player with the ball at the cone passes it to either of the first players positioned at the other two cones, follows the ball past the player who is receiving his pass and approaches the 'static' player at the marker, who plays a 'one-two' pass with him. The player then goes to the end of that team's line to await his next turn. Each player must control the ball to face another line before passing and following it for a one-two with the player at the marker.

Development

⚽ Count the number of successful passes in a given time period.

⚽ Condition play to one- or two-touch control and passing.

⚽ Impose set techniques, such as chip pass, chest or outside of foot control or passing.

⚽ Introduce another ball to increase pressure on the players: the two balls should be kept in motion.

CIRCLE DRILL

Purpose

To develop general passing and controlling techniques, as well as awareness of where to pass the ball.

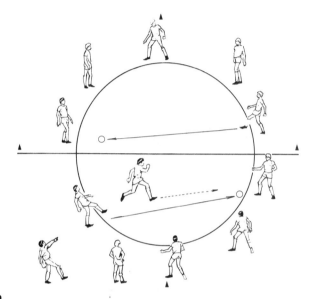

Procedure

A group of players stands around the centre circle with four posts positioned in a 'diamond' pattern approximately 15yds away from the centre lines. One player passes the ball across the circle to the feet of another and immediately follows his pass to change over with the player, who then controls and passes to another player in the circle. Players are not allowed to pass to those on their immediate right or left side. Any player who gives a poor pass, or collides with the ball as they are both travelling across the circle, must sprint around one of the four posts before joining up with the game again.

Development

⚽ The coach can impose certain conditions, such as controlling the ball with the outside of the foot, looking for a bended pass, or only passing with the weaker foot.

⚽ As players improve, the coach can introduce a second and then a third ball, which should be in motion at the same time. Players in this situation should call out an individual's name before passing the ball to him.

THE SQUARE

Purpose

To practise general passing and controlling skills, as well as ball possession and tackling:

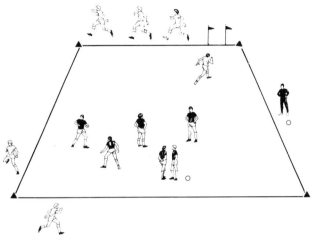

Procedure

In an area 40 x 40yds square, teams play 6 v 6 possession soccer. If a team executes a set number of consecutive passes without the opponents touching the ball, the latter are 'punished' by having to sprint through the 'gate' (made up with posts at one corner), around the square and back inside the gate again to rejoin the game. As soon as one team attains the agreed number of passes the coach blows his whistle and starts timing: the other team is allowed 35 seconds in which to cover the 160yds, and after this the coach whistles a second time to signify 'time up'. As soon as the second whistle blast is signalled, the team inside the square starts another passing sequence to try to achieve the required number of passes to send the opposing team around the square again. The penalised team must set off immediately after the first whistle blast to get as many players back into the square as they can by the time 35 seconds have elapsed.

Development

⚽ Any player who 'gives' the ball away with an unforced error drops out of the game, leaving his team a player short; he can only come back when his team regains ball possession.

⚽ Impose conditions, such as two-touch soccer, or the use of a no tackling rule – only interceptions allowed.

PIG-IN-THE-MIDDLE GAME

Purpose

To develop passing and controlling skills, and ball possession.

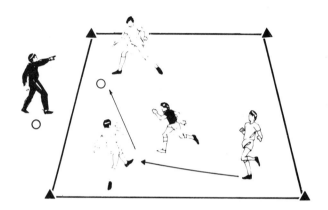

Procedure

In an area 10 x 20 yds, four players play 3 v 1 soccer. The player acting as the defender should wear a brightly coloured shirt or bib for clear identification. The game starts with the three attackers playing two- or three-touch soccer, with the 'pig' trying to get the ball and knock it out of the square. Groups can play for set time limits agreed by the coach, such as 45 seconds, before changing over so that another player becomes the 'pig-in-the-middle' (e.g. the last player to give the ball away). The highest number of consecutive passes attained by a group of three makes them the winners.

Development

- ⚽ The group with the highest number of consecutive passes wins.
- ⚽ The coach can impose conditions, such as one- or two-touch play, passing with the weaker foot where possible, control before passing, etc.
- ⚽ As players progress, groups can be increased to play 4 v 2 soccer in a 20 x 20 yd area, and 6 v 3 in a 30 x 20 yd area, etc.

SWITCH PLAY GAME

Purpose

To practise possession passing and switch passing.

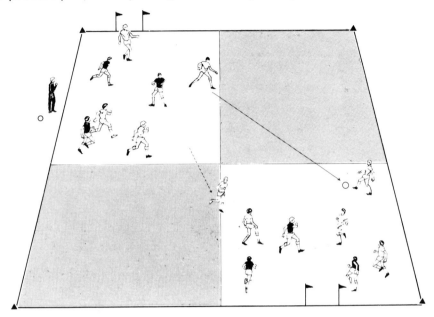

Procedure

Play is in an area approximately 40 x 40 yds square, which is 'quartered', with small goals (without goalkeepers) diagonally opposite each other. Five players play three defenders in one quarter, while 4 v 3 players wait in the other quarter. The five players play possession soccer until they achieve a set number of consecutive passes, e.g. 3–6, whereupon one of them can play a switch pass to a team-mate in the other quarter zone. As soon as the pass it made, the *nearest* attacker sets off to join his team-mates and make it a 5 v 3 game where they try to score in the small goal. Whether they score or not, as soon as the attacking outcome is known, the five attackers start a passing build-up again and look to switch play back to the other quarter zone with a new player running to link up. Change players over.

Development

⚽ The coach can impose conditions, such as one- or two-touch play.

⚽ A set number of passes must be achieved before the switch pass can be made.

OVER-THE-GAP GAME

Purpose

To practise aerial and long passing, possession play and controlling skills.

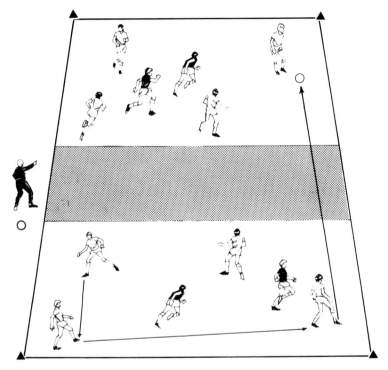

Procedure

An area 60 x 30yds is divided into thirds; four attackers versus two defenders play in each of the final zones. All groups must remain in their own respective zones. On the signal, one of the sets of four attackers plays two-touch soccer while looking for the opportunity to play the ball over the gap to one of the four players in the other end zone. The defending players must try to block or intercept the passes.

Development

⚽ Condition play to two- or one-touch passing, and only allow players to pass a long ball after a certain number of passes has been achieved.

⚽ One or two extra defenders can be situated in the 'no-man's-land', thereby increasing the difficulty for the players in making the long ball pass.

GIVE-AND-GO GAME

Purpose

To develop quick one-two passing and controlling skills.

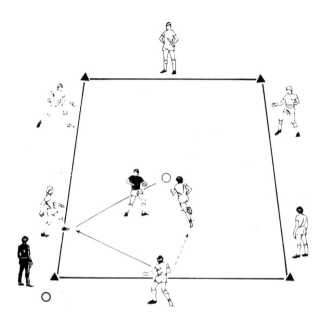

Procedure

Use an area approximately 25 x 15yds. Six players stand outside the rectangle and two inside it, one as a 'give-and-go' player with a ball and the other acting as a defender to intercept the ball. The attacker can screen the ball and pass it to any of the six players situated outside the rectangle, looking for a quick return pass to go past the defender. The six players can play the ball among each other but should take the chance to play it to the player inside the rectangle whenever possible. They are also limited to one- or two-touch soccer. The game is physically strenuous and for this reason the two players inside the area should be changed over at regular intervals.

Development

⚽ Count the number of successful 'give-and-go' passes in the allotted time period.

⚽ The players can be limited to two-, or even one-touch play.

SILENT SOCCER GAME

Purpose

To develop passing, support and possession play, awareness of team-mates and running off the ball.

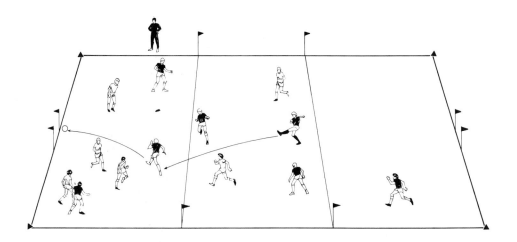

Procedure

In an area approximately 60 x 40 yds wide, two teams play 6 v 6 soccer with no goalkeepers and small goals. A line is marked 15–20 yds from each goal: to score a goal the player must be inside this 'scoring zone'. This will encourage a passing build-up. A spare player who acts as as 'floater' must be a support player for whichever team has possession of the ball, and he does not need to defend. He should wear a different coloured shirt or bib from the rest to help identification. The teams play possession soccer and try to score in the small goal; if any player *calls* for the ball then a free-kick will be given against his team. This will encourage the player 'on-the-ball' to look around quickly before passing.

Development

⚽ The team which scores the most goals wins.

⚽ Impose conditions, such as 'follow your pass', 'control and pass' or look for wall-passing opportunities.

KEEP-BALL GAME

Purpose

To practise basic possession play and penetration.

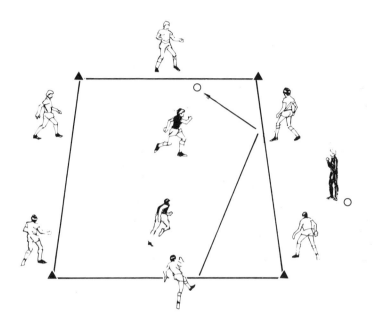

Procedure

Use an area approximately 25 x 15yds wide; six players are stationed around the outside of the rectangle with another two positioned inside. The six players who are not allowed inside the area interpass, while the two defenders who are not allowed outside the area try to intercept the ball. Whichever player has a pass intercepted should change places with one of the defenders. The coach must insist that the ball stays on the move all the time and never becomes stationary.

Development

⚽ Players can be awarded points for maintaining possession of the ball, and extra points if they manage to execute a pass which travels along the length of the rectangle and penetrates the two defenders.

⚽ The coach can impose conditions, such as one-touch passing, passes below knee height, or sole control before passing.

BREAK-OUT GAME

Purpose

To practise general ball possession and timing of passes, and runs off the ball.

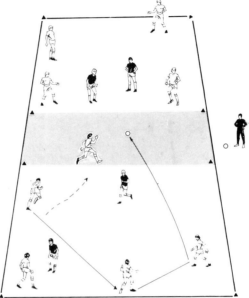

Procedure

Use an area 50 x 20yds, which is divided up so that there is a middle 10 x 20yd zone. 13 players are arranged in the following way: five attackers play possession soccer against two attackers in the end zone. They must achieve a set number of consecutive passes *before* a pass can be played by one of them into the middle 'free zone' for another attacker to break out of his square, collect the ball and run with it to the other end square, linking up with four attackers to play 5 v 2 possession play. These five attackers play as before until they reach the set number of passes, when one player breaks out to link up with the other side again. The defenders are *not* allowed in the middle zone, nor are the attackers allowed to dribble the ball into it or stand waiting in the zone for the ball to arrive. (Offside rule can apply.)

Development

⚽ Players can be conditioned to two-, or even one-touch, play, or the pass played into the central zone must be a specific type, e.g.. wall-pass or chipped pass.

⚽ Extra players can be introduced, or the dimensions of the practice area reduced, to increase pressure on the group.

BLOCKADE GAME

Purpose

To develop penetration play and patient possession soccer.

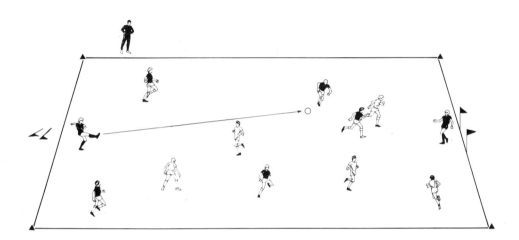

Procedure

In an area approximately 60 x 40yds, six players play six others; goalkeepers should use full-size goals. The rule is this: if a team scores a goal it is *not* allowed to get another until the other team scores one. If the goals are portable, then the players who have lost a goal push their goal off the field and play 'keep-ball' possession soccer for as long as they can before defending their goal when they eventually lose the ball. Their goalkeeper, who has no goal to defend, becomes an outfield player; the team with the goal to defend is not allowed to pass the ball back to the goalkeeper, since this encourages negative play. A free-kick is awarded for infringements of play. The nature of the game is such that one team is encouraged to attack 'all-out', while the other is encouraged to play 'tight' possession soccer.

Development

⚽ The team which has no goal to attack (because it has already scored) may be given an added incentive by awarding points for high numbers of consecutive passes.

⚽ Impose the condition of one- or two-touch play, on one or both teams.

CONDITIONED PASSING GAME

Purpose

To develop general passing and controlling skills, and support play.

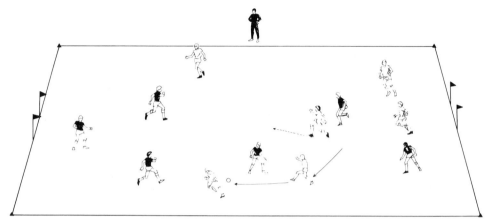

Procedure

The players play 6 v 6 soccer in a 60 x 40yd area. The coach can impose the following conditions to achieve the above aims.

⚽ All passes must be played over a 10yd range; no supporting player must come nearer than this distance to the player on the ball, otherwise a free-kick will be awarded to the other team. The game helps to discourage bunching around the ball.

⚽ If any pass is given in a backward direction, then the next one must be passed first time in a *forward* direction. This will encourage penetration.

⚽ The player who last passed the ball must follow his pass and support the receiver. This prevents each player from standing and admiring his pass, and makes him give immediate support to his team-mates.

⚽ Each player, or specific players nominated by the coach, is only allowed two touches of the ball every time he receives it. This is to encourage players to control and pass the ball accurately at speed.

Development

⚽ All violations of the rules should be punished by the award of a free-kick against the offending team.

⚽ The coach can award points for individuals or teams who are successful in the chosen conditioned play.

CROSS PASSING DRILL

Purpose

To practise varied passing and controlling skills with little space or time available.

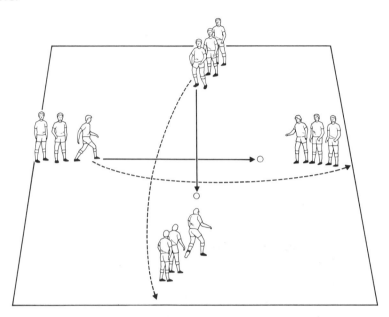

Procedure

Four files of players stand in a cross formation about 10–20 yds apart with the first two players from adjacent files with a ball at their feet. One player passes the ball across to his counterpart opposite, quickly following it across to join the back of the line. The other player, as soon as he spots a gap, passes the ball to his respective side and likewise runs across to join the other group. Each player controls and passes the ball across to his opposite side, keeping two balls on the move at the same time, ensuring that he doesn't hit another player or the other ball as he does so.

Development

⚽ Condition play to two- or even one-touch of the ball as the players improve.

⚽ Have a long and short file where players may be 30 yds and 10 yds apart. The 'long' group chips the ball over the running players as they move through the centre area, while the 'short' group passes along the ground as normal. Change over groups after a period.

B DRIBBLING, SCREENING AND TACKLING

DEFEND YOUR BALL GAME

Purpose

⚽ *For attackers:* to practise basic dribbling, screening and running with the ball.

⚽ *For defenders:* to practise basic tackling techniques.

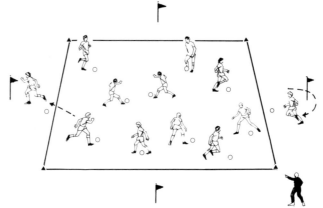

Procedure

Four markers are set up in a diamond shape approximately 15–20yds from a 20 x 20yd square. Each player dribbles his ball under control inside the area while trying to tag another player with his hand. Any player who is tagged or loses control of his ball so that it rolls out of the area must leave it and sprint around a marker before collecting his ball and re-joining the game. As players improve, instead of tagging each other, they can try to tackle and knock other players' balls out of the area, at the same time as controlling and defending their own balls.

Development

⚽ Extra points can be awarded for the successful execution of set techniques, e.g. sole of the foot dribble, or 'nudge' tackle.

⚽ Reduce the area or add more players to create congestion.

⚽ The individual who has knocked the highest number of balls out of the square, or has been forced to do fewest runs for losing control of the ball, wins the game.

GET A BALL GAME

Purpose

To practise dribbling, screening and all-round tackling.

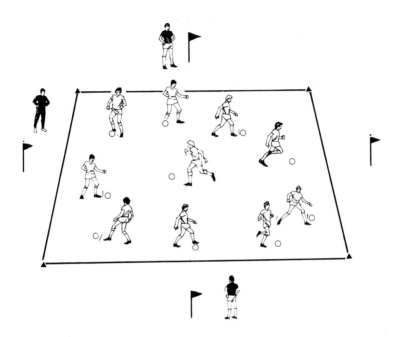

Procedure

The organisation layout is the same as for the previous game. The game starts with each player dribbling his ball inside the square; two other players wait outside without a ball. On the signal the two players enter the area and tackle any player to win a ball for themselves, which they then dribble and 'protect'. If any player is forced to play a ball outside the area, or he loses possession to a tackler, then he must sprint around one of the posts before he can re-enter the square to tackle for a ball. This game is hard work and players will require short rest periods.

Development

⚽ Reduce the size of the area or add more tacklers without balls to increase the degree of difficulty.

⚽ The individual who has won the most tackles, or who has kept possession of his ball for the longest time, wins the game.

Steve McManaman, signed as a gangly schoolboy by Malcolm Cook who was then youth manager at Liverpool, has developed into one of the game's best dribbling exponents, showing deceptive pace, timing and trickery to leave defenders in his wake.

PRESSURE DRILL

Purpose

To practise timing tackles when fatigued, and basic dribbling skills.

Procedure

In an area 20 x 20 yds, two small goals are situated on the corners of one end of a rectangle which has been split into two halves. The squad is broken up into small groups, with one player acting as the defender; the rest line up facing him with a ball at their feet. On the signal each player, in turn, tries to dribble the ball past the defender to score in either of the small goals. The dribbler can only score from the shaded zone, while the defender is allowed to tackle for the ball and knock it out of play from anywhere in the rectangle. As soon as this happens, or if a goal is scored, the next dribbler sets off to attack.

Development

⚽ Use different techniques, e.g. block tackle or change-of-pace dribble.

⚽ Each defender can be given a set time period, e.g. 1 minute, and points awarded for the least or most goals scored in that time.

SLALOM DRILL

Purpose

To practise techniques for speed running with the ball.

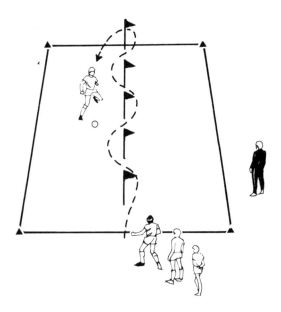

Procedure

Slalom runs are marked with poles or cones, in an area approximately 25 x 10 yds. The squad is arranged in small groups behind the slalom, with the leading player having the ball. On the signal, the player proceeds to run and dribble the ball through the slalom, finishing with a straight speed run and placing his foot on the ball so that it is stationary for the next player. This continues until each member of the group has had a go. Any player who misses a pole or comes out of the zone must return to the last pole before re-starting his run.

Development

⚽ Perform varying techniques or 'tricks' on the ball with both feet.

⚽ Increase the number of runs.

⚽ Increase the difficulty of the slalom by adding more posts.

⚽ Give points to whichever group completes a set number of runs in the fastest time.

Ryan Giggs has a maturity beyond his years and a wide range of attacking skills, none more than his ability to dribble past trailing defenders with devastating effect.

1 v 1 GAME

Purpose

⚽ *For attackers:* to practise dribbling, screening and turning with the ball to beat a player.

⚽ *For defenders:* to practise jockeying for the ball and various tackling techniques.

Procedure

The squad is divided into small groups, each of which is split up into two teams to play in an area 20 x 15 yds, with a small goal at both ends. Players in the two teams are numbered. The first from each play 1 v 1: the player with the ball tries to dribble past his opponent and score by pushing the ball through the goal. If the player scores he then immediately defends his goal against the next opponent while the beaten defender retreats behind his own goal to await his turn to defend or attack again. If the defender wins the ball he can score in the opponent's goal – the more successful he is at dribbling, the longer he will be in action. If the ball goes out of bounds, it should be returned by other players so that play is continuous.

Development

⚽ The individual who scores the most goals wins the game.

⚽ Extra points are awarded for a particular technique which is performed successfully, e.g. front foot tackle, or beating a player by playing the ball past him on one side and collecting it on the other.

CONDITIONED DRIBBLE GAME

Purpose

⚽ *For attackers:* to practise dribbling, screening and turning with the ball to beat a player.

⚽ *For defenders:* to practise intercepting, jockeying and tackling for the ball.

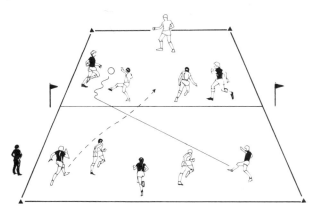

Procedure

An area approximately 40 x 30 yds wide is marked out and split into two halves. The game is 5 v 5, with each team having three defenders and two attackers who are restricted to their own half of the area. The game begins with one of the back players dribbling and later passing the ball with the other back players. They have to get the ball up to one of their two colleagues in the opposite half who, in turn, look for opportunities to screen and dribble the ball past opponents until one of them carries the ball under control over the end line to score a point. The attackers cannot pass the ball *over* the end line; also, defenders must make their tackles *before* the attacker reaches the end line. The sets of players should be changed around so that all experience dribbling and tackling practice.

Development

⚽ Limit the number of passes that attackers can make to encourage dribbling and tackling.

⚽ Give attackers or defenders extra points for successful displays of set techniques, e.g. tackling with the weaker foot only, or turning with the ball to beat a player.

⚽ The team with more 'goals', or fewer against them, wins the game.

TAKE-OVER DRILL

Purpose

To practise take-overs while running with the ball.

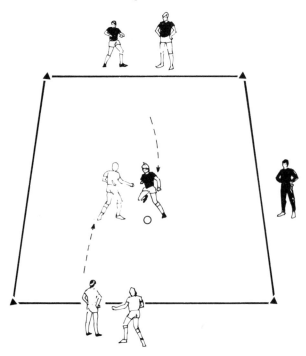

Procedure

In an area approximately 25 x 10yds, two files of players face each other; one of the leading players has the ball. On the coach's signal the player runs with the ball under control towards one side of the next player on the opposite line. As he approaches with the ball, the receiving player performs a take-over and carries the ball on to the next player on the other side, who then takes it from him. The drill continues in this way until all the players have had a turn.

Development

⚽ On a signal, the take-over player pretends to take the ball but actually performs a 'dummy' manoeuvre, leaving the dribbling player to carry on with the ball.

⚽ Give points to the group that completes a set number of runs with the ball in the fastest time.

 **CROSSING AND HEADING**

KEEP-UP DRILL

Purpose

To practise controlled heading techniques.

Procedure

The squad splits into small groups that compete against each other in an area 10 x 10 yds square. Players line up in two files facing each other, about 2 or 3 yds apart. The first player tosses the ball up in the air and heads it to the first player on the *opposite* side, while moving in the direction of the ball to join the end of the far line and await his turn to head the ball again. The next player heads the ball to the player opposite him and moves to the back of that file, and so the sequence continues. The players keep the ball in the air with their heads only.

Development

⚽ Count the total number of consecutive headers.

⚽ The coach can ask players to perform two successive headers before playing the ball to the next player.

⚽ A static player can stand between the files so that all headers have to be played over him.

Teddy Sheringham is especially effective in converting crosses with his head but also has the ability to move to the flanks and return the compliment by crossing accurately for waiting colleagues in dangerous positions.

NON-STOP ATTACK

Purpose

To practise crossing and heading techniques.

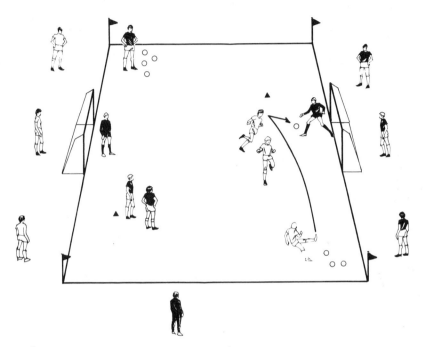

Procedure

The squad is divided into two teams, each with six players and one goalkeeper, in an area 20 x 40yds wide. Three players act as retrievers, two as attackers looking for headers, and the last one from the team crosses the ball. The game starts with one of the wingers crossing the ball for the two attackers to come to the near and far goal post areas to head for goal directly, or to set up one-touch shooting chances. As soon as the header, or shot, is taken the winger on the other side of the area crosses for his two attackers who must start from, and return to, their cone each time. The players change over after a set time period.

Development

⚽ Count the total number of headed goals per individual and group.

⚽ Allow the goalkeepers to come out for crosses.

⚽ Add a defender to challenge for the ball.

THROW- OR VOLLEY-HEAD-CATCH

Purpose

To practise general heading skills.

Procedure

Two teams play in an area 40 x 30 yds, with full-size goals at each corner. The game starts with a player throwing the ball into the air for a team-mate to head so that another team-mate can catch it and restart the throw-head-catch sequence again. The player about to throw the ball must not be obstructed by opponents; however, once the ball is in the air they can jump to challenge for the ball. A free throw is awarded to a team when one of their opponents fails to head a thrown ball. If goalkeepers are used, they should be limited to their own goal lines.

Development

⚽ The coach can introduce a volley-head-catch sequence where the player volleys the ball from his hands instead of throwing it.

⚽ Allow players to double-head the ball when convenient, rather than catching it.

⚽ Count the total number of headed goals.

CLEAR THE DECKS GAME

Purpose

To develop crossing techniques
and defensive heading skills.

Procedure

The squad splits into three groups of players. One group acts as ball retrievers, another as defenders and the last group has two players as attackers and two as crossers. The wingers, who have a good supply of balls, each cross a ball in turn into the penalty area, but *not* into the goal area which is 'no-man's-land'. The four defenders, lacking a goalkeeper, try to head the ball out of the marked out area while the two attackers attempt to score with headers or challenge for the ball. If the defenders fail to use sufficient power to 'clear the decks' so that the ball does not land past the penalty area line, then the two attackers who are positioned outside the penalty area can combine with the attackers and try to score while the four defenders come out quickly to block the shot. If the ball is cleared by a header which lands past the line, then the ball is returned to the wingers who cross alternately.

Development

⚽ Count the total number of headed clearances and goals scored against the defenders.

⚽ Extend the danger zone so that headers need to be more powerful.

⚽ Add another attacker to the penalty box.

END-TO-END HEADING GAME

Purpose

To develop crossing techniques and attacking/defending heading skills.

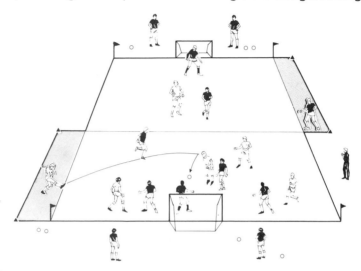

Procedure

The squad divides into two groups, each with a goalkeeper who is always in action. The game is played in an area approximately 40 x 50 yds wide, which has goals at each end plus a channel for a winger from each team to play inside. The teams play two-touch soccer and try to get the ball quickly to their own winger, who is restricted to the attacking half of the field and cannot be tackled in his channel. The winger crosses the ball for attackers to attempt to score with headers while being challenged by defenders. At the conclusion of every attack the goalkeeper rolls the ball to one of his team-mates who has just been defending and his team tries to get the ball to their winger so that they can attack the other goal. Corners can be played, as can throw-ins and free-kicks. The goalkeeper may be restricted, initially, to his goal line.

Development

⚽ Count the total number of successful headed clearances and goals scored.

⚽ Allow the winger to move out of his channel and another attacker to move into it to cross the ball.

⚽ Allow the goalkeeper to take crosses.

BOXED-IN GAME

Purpose

To develop crossing and general heading skills.

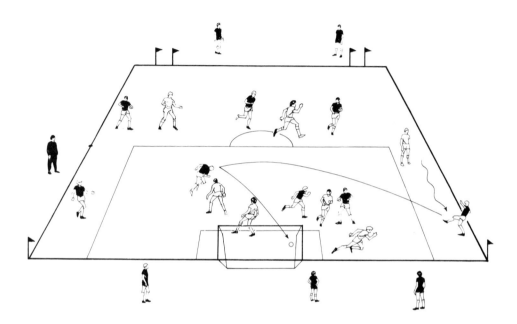

Procedure

Four defenders play three attackers: they are all restricted to the penalty box, and there is no goalkeeper. Outside the box five attackers play against three defenders with the restriction that these eight players are *not* allowed in the box. The five attackers play possession soccer and try to set up crosses from varied positions into the box for their three team-mates to score with headers, while defenders try to clear the ball through one of the two small goals at the end of the field. The number of players can be altered depending on whether the coach wishes to emphasise attacking or defensive heading, or put more pressure on the crossers.

Development

⚽ Count the number of headed goals or successful clearances.

⚽ The coach can condition the game so that wingers must play first-time crosses.

WAVES OF ATTACK

Purpose

To practise varied crossing and heading situations in attack.

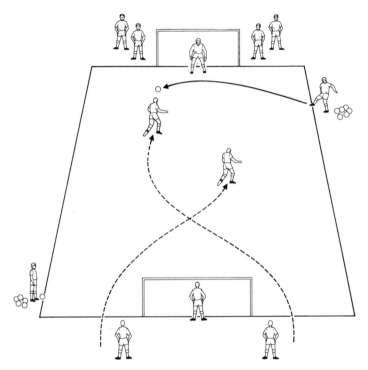

Procedure

Eight players form up in pairs at the sides of two portable goals about 20 yds apart, each defended by a goalkeeper. Two players stand on opposite flanks with a good supply of balls. The first pair of attackers attacks the other goal by a cross-over run to look for the cross to the near or far post region, where they try to score with a headed goal. As soon as the attack ends, another pair of attackers immediately comes from the other end to look for a cross, and thus the practice ebbs and flows from end to end.

Development

⚽ Ask the servers to cross a specific type of service for a set period, e.g. far post, diving header at near post, etc.

⚽ Add a defender to give him defensive practice or to make it more realistic and difficult for the attackers.

D SHOOTING

TWO-TOUCH SHOOTING GAME

Purpose

To develop basic shooting techniques.

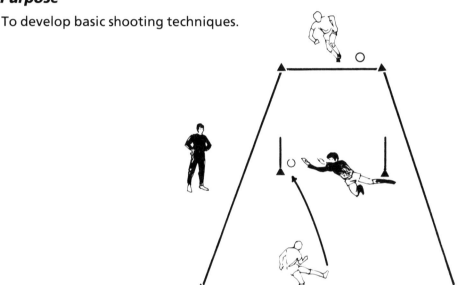

Procedure

The squad is split into groups of three, with one player acting as goalkeeper. The drill takes place in an area 40 x 15 yds wide. Posts are placed in the ground 8 yds apart, half-way up the length of the area. Each player is allowed two touches of the ball before he shoots at goal; if the goalkeeper saves the ball, or if it travels past the goal, it is collected by the other player who then shoots as the goalkeeper turns to face the shot. The players change over after a set time period and scores are recorded.

Development

⚽ The players can practise varying techniques, such as volleys or swerved shots.

⚽ Another player may be introduced to act as a defender and put in challenges to add more realism to the game.

LAY-OFF DRILL

Purpose

To develop varied shooting techniques while on the run.

Procedure

The squad is organised into two small groups, one of which acts as ball retrievers, while the other group practises. The drill takes place in the penalty box area where a goalkeeper defends the goal. One player stands in the 'D'; the other players, each with a ball, stand in a file facing him, approximately 20yds away. The first player in the line passes the ball to the feet of the player in the 'D', who proceeds to 'lay' it off for the former to shoot at goal. The 'lay-off' player then goes to either cone A or cone B to collect a ball from the retrievers before returning down the side to join the file and await his turn. The player who has just shot at goal becomes the next 'lay-off' player and faces the second oncoming player. In this way, each player shoots, and acts as the wall-player.

Development

⚽ Each group is timed for a set period and the scores tallied up.

⚽ The coach can impose certain conditions, such as shooting with the weaker foot, or volleys from the 'lay-off' player flicking the ball up for another player to hit at goal, or long-range shots. Record the number of goals scored in a given time period.

Eric Cantona brings new dimensions to the game through his wonderfully imaginative play. He is renowned for his quest for perfection and extra practice time mainly dedicated to finishing. His all-round excellence and execution of stunning goals are testimony to this practice.

CHANGE-OVER GAME

Purpose

To create and take shooting opportunities.

Procedure

Two teams (A and B) use an area 60 x 30yds. A goal, 8yds wide, is marked with posts and defended by a goalkeeper. Play is 5 (A) v 4 (B) in one half of the area — A's fifth player is positioned in the other half. B's five attackers make use of the extra player and combine to shoot at goal. When the ball enters the other half B's four defenders join up with their colleague and become the attackers, while four players from team B move into that half to defend. This leaves one player behind and creates the 5 v 4 situation once again. As soon as the ball enters the other half, the nearest defenders must come out quickly to block the shot.

Development

⚽ To encourage shooting, the players play one- or two-touch soccer.

⚽ Shots which hit the target after a first-time strike gain extra points.

SHOOTING ON THE TURN GAME

Purpose

To develop players' ability to shoot in turning situations.

Procedure

The game takes place from the width of the penalty area up to the half-way line where two small goals are placed on the sides of the area. The squad is split up into three teams with one goalkeeper; one team acts as ball retrievers. The attacking team has two players who are restricted to the penalty box – the other attackers are not allowed inside. The two defenders stand inside the goal area while the others play outside the penalty box. The out-field players attempt to play the ball to one of their colleagues in the box who, in turn, tries to turn and shoot or lay the ball off for his team-mate to shoot first time. One of the defenders may leave the penalty area to make a challenge when the ball enters the box, while the other blocks the goal. If the defenders win the ball they attempt to play it through one of the small goals.

Development

⚽ The coach can impose the condition that the two attackers are only allowed one pass inside the penalty box.

⚽ Initially, the coach can restrict the defenders so that only one can challenge the two attackers – the other must stand on the goal line with the goalkeeper.

⚽ The coach can award extra points for the use of difficult skills which result in a goal, e.g. volleys or half-volleys, shots on the turn, and 'bicycle' kicks.

COLLECT AND SHOOT GAME

Purpose

To develop quick breaks and create early shooting situations.

Procedure

The squad is divided up into three small groups: one of the groups retrieves the balls, while the other two play attack versus defence in an area stretching from the goal line to the half-way line. A supply of balls is left in the centre circle. The game starts with the goalkeeper and all the other players stationed inside the penalty area. The coach calls a player's name and he runs to collect a ball and dribble it forwards, while the other players combine with him to try to get a shot at goal. If they win the ball, the defenders play it to one of the retrievers on the half-way line.

Development

⚽ The coach can put increased demands on certain players by regularly nominating them to collect the ball.

⚽ Each group is given a set time limit and goals are recorded.

⚽ The coach can impose conditions, such as two-touch soccer, forward passes only, or first-time shots only.

ON-TARGET GAME

Purpose

To develop controlled
shooting skills.

Procedure

The squad is divided into three groups, that retrieve the ball or defend/
attack in the game. The game is played in the same area as for 'Collect and
shoot', with two small goals on the half-way line. The coach has a few balls
in the centre circle; when he passes a ball to a player this signals that the
team with the ball must attack and attempt a shot at goal, while the other
team must defend and try eventually to play the ball through one of the
small goals. If the defenders manage to do this, then they receive the next
service from the coach and attack the goal, while the other team now
defends. However, should the attacking team get a shot on target they
receive the *next* service, or if they manage to score they receive the next *two*
services.

Development

⚽ The coach can 'punish' teams that shoot inaccurately when not under
   pressure, or that fail to accept shooting chances, by giving the next
   service to the other team.

⚽ The coach can impose one- or two-touch play to quicken shooting.

⚽ Groups change around after a set period of time and scores are
   recorded.

PRESSURE SHOOTING DRILL

Purpose

To develop quick-reaction shooting skills.

Procedure

The squad is divided into three groups and a goalkeeper. The coach stands outside the penalty box and half-circle and serves balls into the area for players to shoot quickly at goal. The service is indiscriminate and whichever player gets to the ball first shoots, or passes to a team-mate who must shoot *first time*. The service must be continuous and each team is timed for a set duration before changing over its role. The coach can serve a variety of techniques, such as the volley. The team which does not have ball possession must challenge immediately to prevent shots and force shooting errors.

Development

The coach records the teams' scores and gives added 'bonus' points for players who perform difficult techniques, such as overhead shots at goal.

LONG-RANGE GAME

Purpose

To develop long-range shooting skills.

Procedure

In an area approximately 50 x 40yds, set up two portable goals on the end lines and single posts on the half-way line. The squad is divided into three groups and two goalkeepers: one group retrieves while the other two practise in the area. The teams play 3 v 1 in each half of the area; the attackers set up shooting chances for each other, while the one defender challenges for the ball. The three players can pass the ball to their isolated team-mate in the other half but can only receive return passes in their own half. The advanced player can look for deflections or 'knockdowns' from the longer shots to follow in and score. The game fluctuates from end to end, with the goalkeeper serving the ball for a team-mate to attack the other end as soon as a shot is hit at goal.

Development

⚽ Conditions such as one- or two-touch play can be introduced.

⚽ Other attacking and defending players can be added.

⚽ The coach can allow any of the three players to pass the ball to a team-mate in the other half and break forwards to shoot at goal.

SURPRISE SHOOTING GAME

Purpose

To escape tight marking and to take unexpected shooting chances.

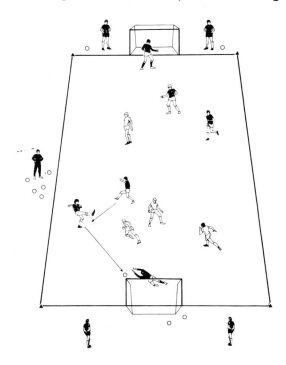

Procedure

The squad is split into three groups, with two goalkeepers in action throughout the game – two portable goals are placed on the end lines. The coach receives balls from the servers to keep the game continuous. He serves the ball to a player whose team attacks and tries to score, while the other team defends, although if they win the ball they can attack. As soon as an attack is completed, the coach should serve the ball to the other team, thus ensuring that play is end-to-end.

Development

⚽ The coach should occasionally play the ball to players in situations where they will have to react quickly.

⚽ The coach can impose conditions, such as only allowing one or two players from each team to score.

⚽ The scores should, as always, be recorded.

TACTICAL GAMES

CONDITIONED OFF-THE-BALL GAME

Purpose

To develop off-the-ball attacking play.

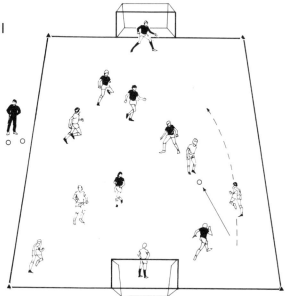

Procedure

In an area approximately 60 x 40 yds, the squad plays 6 v 6 soccer, with goalkeepers and portable goals. The coach imposes certain conditions on the players for a short duration, which if violated are punished with free-kicks. Some conditions include:

⚽ each player must overlap the colleague to whom he passes the ball

⚽ specific players must get into and attack the space behind the rear defenders when the ball is in a certain position.

Development

⚽ The coach can teach players making the runs forwards to either run *in front* of defenders to draw them out of position, or to run *behind* to the blind side where it is more difficult to be seen and marked.

⚽ Extra points can be awarded to players who perform off-the-ball movements successfully.

CLOSING-DOWN GAME

Purpose

To develop defensive closing-down play.

Procedure

On an area 60 x 40yds the squad plays 7 v 7 soccer, with goalkeepers and portable goals. The coach imposes the condition that the *nearest* defender to the player with the ball each time shouts 'One!' to indicate clearly to all that it is his responsibility to close the attacker down, which he attempts as soon as he has shouted. If he fails to do this he is punished with a free-kick against his team. As the defensive organisation improves the next player in a covering position behind 'One' shouts 'Two!' to indicate that his role is to cover.

Development

⚽ The coach can teach players to close down the correct distance and angle.

⚽ Players who close down effectively and prevent the ball going forwards, or actually win the ball, can be awarded extra points by the coach.

Denis Bergkamp blends good technical skills with their intelligent application in the game. He gives his team tactical options by his shrewdness and ability to time his runs into the attacking area at the most opportune time.

MAN-MARKING GAME

Purpose

To learn how to mark closely and how to escape this marking; also to practise the 'sweeper's' role.

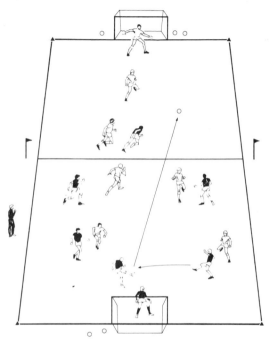

Procedure

The teams play in an area approximately 60 x 40 yds, with the condition that each player in each team is responsible for marking and tackling his own particular opponent. If any player marks or tackles somebody other than the player he is delegated to watch, then a free-kick will be awarded against him. Each team has a 'free-man' or 'sweeper' who is restricted to playing in his own half of the field and to two- or one-touch soccer. He can also cover his team-mates and intercept or tackle in his own half *any* attackers who have broken free from their markers.

Development

⚽ Restrict the sweeper to one-touch play only.

⚽ Allow the sweeper to 'break' over the half-way line and into the opponents' half: the man-markers can leave their own opponents to challenge him if they feel it necessary.

FOUR-GOAL GAME

Purpose

To develop passing and switching play in attack, and cover and balance in defence.

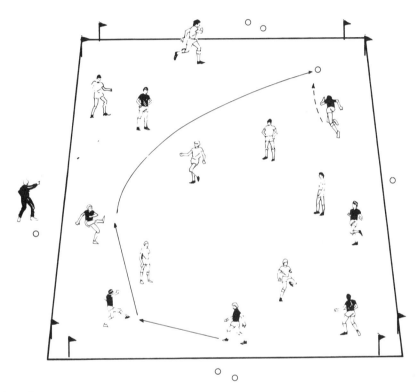

Procedure

An area approximately 60 x 60yds square is used; four small goals are placed at each corner. Goalkeepers do not play; each team defends two goals at one end and attacks the other two at the far end. The players play possession soccer and attempt to 'pull' the bulk of the defenders over to defend one goal before switching the ball suddenly towards the less well-guarded goal, and trying to score there.

Development

⚽ Play one- or two-touch soccer.

⚽ The coach can award extra points for goals which come directly from the team switching play.

KEEP THE PRISONER

Purpose

To develop defensive closing-down, cover and balance.

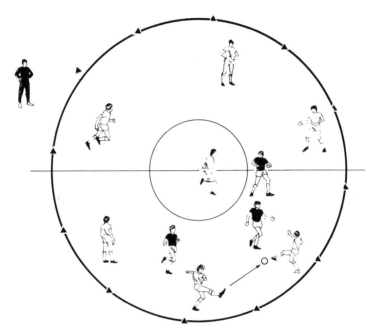

Procedure

A large circle approximately 50 yds in diameter is marked around the centre circle with cones. One attacker is restricted to the area inside the centre circle, while his colleagues play 6 v 3 soccer in the outer area. The six attackers play possession soccer and try to finish with a pass to the colleague inside the circle; the three defenders work to prevent them doing this. The defenders can run across and through the inner circle; however, they are now allowed to stop and intercept passes inside this area. Players change over after a set time period.

Development

⚽ Initially, do not allow attackers to play the ball above knee-height, but as defenders improve withdraw this restriction.

⚽ Add more or fewer players, depending on the success of the game.

⚽ Time each trio of defenders for a given period: the group which concedes the least number of passes wins the game.

BUILD-UP GAME

Purpose

To develop controlled passing play from the back region of the team up to the front.

Procedure

On half a full-size pitch, the squad is split up into defenders and attackers in an 8 v 6 situation, with a goalkeeper, and two players restricted to being able to move only *along* the half-way line. The game starts with the goalkeeper rolling the ball out to a player; the team then interpasses until one of them carries the ball at his feet *unopposed* over the half-way line. The players on the half-way line can shuttle across the line to challenge any players approaching with the ball.

Passes cannot be played *over* the half-way line for players to run on to: the attacker must dribble the ball over to score a point. If an attack breaks down the ball must go back to the goalkeeper and the patient passing build-up must start again.

Development

⚽ Condition play to one- or two-touch passing.

⚽ Add another defender to make passing more difficult.

LL-UP AND ALL-BACK GAME

Purpose

To develop compact team play.

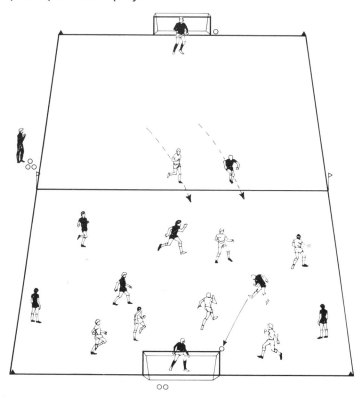

Procedure

In an area approximately 60 x 40yds, with portable goals on the end lines and a half-way line marked on the area, two teams play soccer with the following condition of play: for a goal to count, the entire team must be over the half-way line and into the opponents' half of the area when the final header or shot is struck.

Development

A team can be awarded *two* goals if they score with their players over the half-way line *and* if they catch 'stragglers' from the opposition who have not managed to get back into their defensive half of the area when the goal is scored. Attackers who cannot get back are punished by a free-kick being given to the opposition from the point at which they were caught.

RE-START GAME

Purpose

To develop the squad's re-start organisational play.

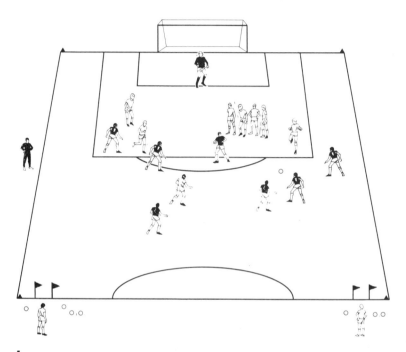

Procedure

The squad plays attack versus defence in one half of the field, with the distribution of players depending on whether the coach is working on attacking or defensive play. Two small goals are placed to the sides of the half-way line; two players, who have a supply of balls, act as servers and retrievers behind these goals. The attackers receive the ball from one of the servers and proceed to attack the goal; the defenders try to protect their goal and win the ball, playing it as quickly as possible through either of the two smaller goals. The coach blows his whistle to indicate real or imaginary offences which result in free-kicks, corner kicks or throw-ins for the attacking team. This gives both attackers and defenders practice in dealing with re-start situations.

Development

The coach can award extra points for 'special' ploys which are demonstrated successfully.

BENCH PASSING CIRCUIT

Purpose

To practise short passing and control techniques.

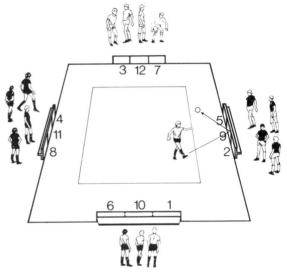

Procedure

Four benches are laid on the floor and numbered, as indicated, from 1 to 12. A small inner square, or rectangle, is marked on the floor, approximately 15 yds from the benches. The group is organised into two small teams and one player from each team stands in the inner square or rectangle with a ball at his feet. On the signal a player moves forwards and passes the ball against the bench from 1 to 2, 2 to 3, 3 to 4, and so on until he reaches 12. Each player must hit the numbered area, making sure that he passes the ball from *inside* the inner area every time and always controls the ball *outside* it before bringing the ball back to face the next number.

Development

⚽ The team which completes the circuit in the fastest time wins.

⚽ The players can be conditioned to use set techniques, such as weaker foot to control or pass, outside of foot only, sole of foot control, etc.

⚽ Two players, one from each team, can compete against each other: one moves from 1 to 12 while the other moves in the opposite direction and passes from 12 to 1. Whichever player finishes first wins.

SOCCER SQUASH

Purpose

To develop driving, volleying and control techniques.

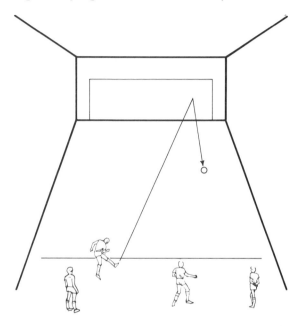

Procedure

A long goal, about 10 x 2yds high, is marked on a wall and a 'shooting line' marked on the floor approximately 15–20yds away from the wall. The group is organised into two small teams numbered from 1 onwards. Each player from each team drives the ball into goal in rotation. After a player has struck the ball at the goal, the next player, behind the line, controls the rebound off the wall before he in turn drives the ball at the wall. Any player who misses the target, hits the ball with insufficient power, or fails to control the ball properly either loses a point for his team or drops out of the game; play re-starts with the next player playing the ball.

Development

⚽ The coach can impose conditions, such as use of weaker foot only, flick ball up into the air before volleying at goal, control ball while in the air, etc.

⚽ The coach can impose a time limit during which groups have to attain as many drive passes as they can.

BENCH SOCCER

Purpose

To develop control, and short volleying techniques.

Procedure

Double benches, or a low rope or net, are used to section the court into equal halves. The players are split into teams and the game is played with a lightweight ball. The game starts with one player, who is positioned at the back of the court, tossing the ball up in front of himself and gently lobbing it with his foot over the benches and into the opponents' side of the court. The ball is only allowed to bounce once on the floor before being 'juggled' in the air with head, foot or body: it must be returned within a set number of touches into the opponents' side again. (Players are not allowed to volley in a downward direction.) Whichever team allows the ball to touch the floor more than once or fails to return it over the bench and into the opponents' area loses a point.

Development

⚽ The first team to reach a set number of points wins the game.

⚽ The coach can impose the condition that only one particular player from each team can return the ball, or the ball can only be returned with the weaker foot.

CRAB SOCCER

Purpose

To develop strength, agility, control and volleying techniques.

Procedure

A small group from the squad is split into two teams that play in an area with benches, acting as goals, at each end. The players move around backwards, sideways or forwards in 'crab' fashion, keeping hands and at least one foot in contact with the floor to interpass, head, dribble and shoot to score by hitting the bench. The goalkeeper is allowed to sit or kneel on the mat and a penalty kick will be awarded if he gets up from the stated position. The other players are likewise punished if they get up from the floor, handle the ball or seek to gain an unfair advantage.

Development

⚽ The team scoring the most goals wins the game.

⚽ The coach can give extra points for goals scored by volleying the ball, thereby encouraging specific skills.

HEAD TENNIS

Purpose

To develop controlled heading.

Procedure

A net or rope approximately 5 ft high is placed half-way across a 30 x 30 yd court, and the game is played with a lightweight ball. The group is split into two teams that are stationed either side of the net. One player at the back of the court starts the game by tossing the ball into the air and heading it over the net into the other half of the court. The ball is only allowed one bounce on the floor; players must juggle the ball into the air with their feet for three successive headers from three different players before returning it over the net. A team loses a point if the ball bounces twice on their side, fails to go over the net and into the opponents' court, or is not headed by three players in succession. Teams scoring a point retain the service.

Development

The team to score more points wins.

HIT-AND-RUN

Purpose

To develop control and drive passing techniques.

Procedure

Two players, wearing distinctive coloured bibs or shorts to make them easily identifiable, act as 'shooters' and interpass to try to shoot and hit the other players below their knees with the ball. The latter aim to dodge and evade the ball; they can use their hands to protect themselves if shots come at their face – for safety purposes it is advisable that a lightweight ball is used. Any player hit with the ball either loses a point or drops out of the game. The 'shooters' are given a time period in which to hit as many players and score as many points as they can.

Development

To make it more difficult for the 'shooters' the coach can impose a one- or two-touch condition, or he may only allow them to shoot with their weaker foot.

CHANGE SOCCER

Purpose

To develop general passing, control and awareness of the ball.

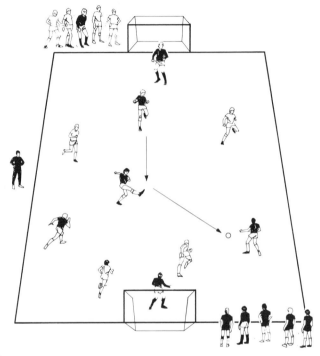

Procedure

Benches or small goals are placed at either end of the indoor area and the squad is split up into four smaller teams, with coloured shirts or bibs for identification. The teams sit in the corners and each is given a number, 1–4. When the coach calls out two numbers the relevant teams play soccer for a set period, and only retire to their own corners when other numbers are called. As soon as they hear their numbers, teams immediately defend the *nearer* goal and try to score at the other end. The coach, if he wishes, can keep both goalkeepers in action all the time.

Development

⚽ Teams can be handicapped by having to play with a player short, or they may be conditioned to one- or two-touch play.

⚽ The team to score the most goals or win the most games wins the competition.

CHAIN RUN

Purpose

To develop dribbling techniques and agility.

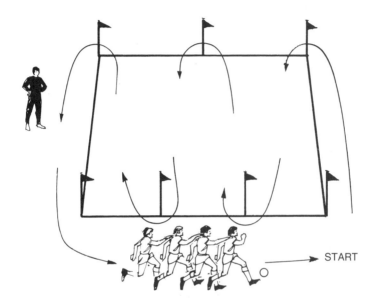

Procedure

An area approximately 20 x 20yds square is marked out, with posts positioned around the edges of the square. The squad is broken up into small groups; group players form a chain by holding the backs of each other's shorts. The leading player dribbles the ball around the circuit while the rest, keeping linked-up, move behind him. When the run is completed the dribbler halts the ball and moves to link up at the rear of the 'chain'. The front player then dribbles the ball and the pattern continues until the entire group completes the run. If a team loses control of the ball, the players must retrieve it, maintaining the chain formation, and re-start the run where they lost control; similarly, if the chain 'breaks', players must return to their original positions.

Development

The coach can create competitions which keep to a set time schedule, increase the number of runs, or increase the difficulty of the circuit.

TUNNEL BALL RELAY

Purpose

To develop short passing, running with the ball and agility work.

Procedure

The squad splits up into small groups of players that compete against each other in an area 20 x 10yds, with a marker post at each end. Players line up in a file behind a post with their legs opened wide to form a tunnel. On the signal, the first player in the team turns to face the rest of his players and push-passes the ball through the tunnel. The end player in the file then controls it before dribbling it around the post at the other end of the area, returning to the front of the file and passing it through the tunnel for the next player. This continues until the last member of the team has finished, or the team has completed a set number of runs.

Development

⚽ The winner is the fastest team or the team which completes the most runs in a given time period.

⚽ The coach can impose conditions, such as passing and running with the ball, using only the weaker foot, etc.

STEAL-A-BALL

Purpose

To develop dribbling techniques and awareness of the ball.

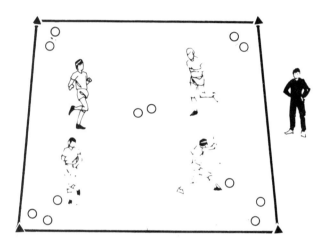

Procedure

An area 20 x 20yds square, with cones at each corner, is marked out. Four players are positioned at each cone and 12 balls are bunched together in the centre of the square. On the signal, the players run to the centre, dribble a ball back to their corner and place it by the cone. The first player to have *four* balls at his corner wins the game. Players cannot tackle each other but they are allowed to 'steal' balls from other players' corners when they are out of their areas.

Development

To prevent the game from becoming too lengthy, the coach can count the number of balls at each player's cone after a given period of time: the player with the highest total wins the game.

 **GOALKEEPING**

SHUTTLE GOALKEEPING DRILL

Purpose

To practise various handling techniques.

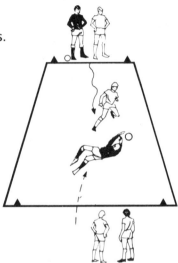

Procedure

Players line up in files facing each other approximately 20 yds apart, with a goalkeeper in each file. Cones are placed on the end lines to act as goals. While the rest of the players pass and follow the ball to the back of the line, the goalkeepers field the ball with their hands before rolling it to the feet of the next player from the opposite side and then following across. In this way the goalkeeper can join in a normal drill activity and practise his own specific techniques, while the other players practise their own particular skills.

Development

⚽ The coach can ask players to try to push the ball past the goalkeeper to score in the goals. The goalkeeper attempts to dive and save the ball each time.

⚽ The coach can direct players to give specific practice to the goalkeepers, e.g. play the ball high in the air for the goalkeeper to catch, drive the ball hard at his chest, or attempt to dribble the ball around the goalkeeper.

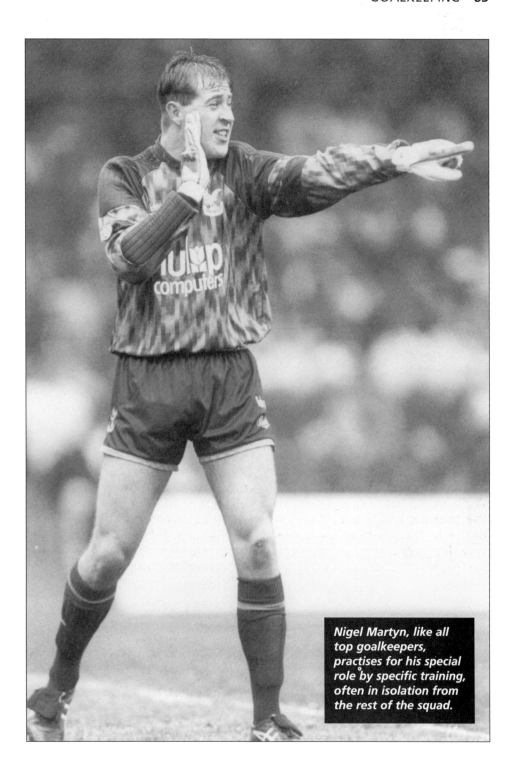

Nigel Martyn, like all top goalkeepers, practises for his special role by specific training, often in isolation from the rest of the squad.

SHOT STOPPING AND DISTRIBUTION GAME

Purpose

To develop positional sense and to practise handling and ball distribution.

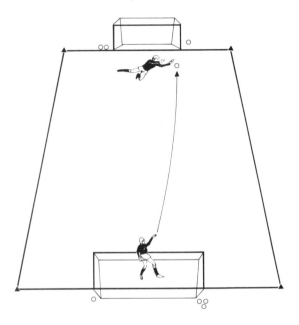

Procedure

In an area approximately 30 x 20 yds wide, two portable goals are placed on the end lines, with both goalkeepers facing each other and having a good supply of balls placed at the back of each goal. The first goalkeeper starts by rolling the ball along the ground to try to score in the other goal, while the opposite goalkeeper positions himself to save the ball. The ball should be played backwards and forwards as quickly as possible so that the pressure on both goalkeepers is continuous. As the practice develops the goalkeepers can use overarm throws or volley/half-volley kicks to try to score.

Development

⚽ Record which goalkeeper scores more goals in a given period.

⚽ The goals can be moved nearer to each other or further apart to make saving in the former or distribution in the latter more difficult.

⚽ A player can be placed within 10 yds of each goal; he is allowed to score from any mishandling by the goalkeeper.

CROSS BALL GAME

Purpose

To give the goalkeepers practice in dealing with crosses from the flanks.

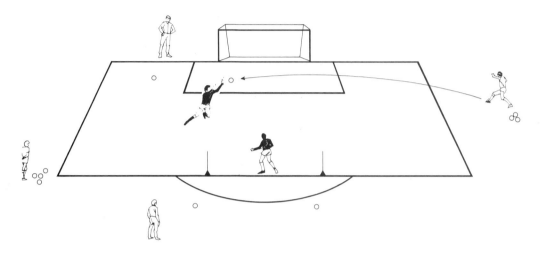

Procedure

A makeshift goal is set up directly opposite the permanent field goal about 20 yds away. The two goalkeepers defend the goals, two wingers cover the flanks and one or two retrievers stand behind the goals. The wingers, who have a supply of balls, cross them into the 6-yd box in turn for the goalkeepers to catch or punch away to safety. If a goalkeeper catches the ball he immediately throws it to the winger on the opposite side, who then crosses it to his goalkeeper, thus maintaining continuity. After a time the same or other wingers should cross the ball from different flanks to give the goalkeepers practice in taking crosses from both flanks.

Development

⚽ The coach can direct the servers to play specific types of cross to give the goalkeepers more difficult shots to deal with, e.g. leg inswinging crosses, near or far post balls or occasional driven shots.

⚽ The coach can add a defender and one attacker to pose extra problems before adding more to the practice.

TRIANGLE DRILL

Purpose

To develop agility, positional sense and shot stopping.

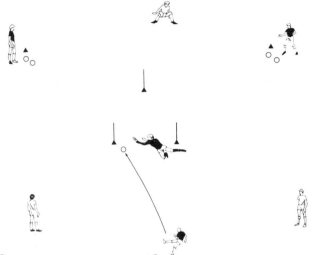

Procedure

A three-goal triangle of normal full-size goal dimensions is set up on a good diving area. Three cones are positioned about 15–20 yds away facing the centre of the goals. One player stands at each cone, with at least two balls, while three retrievers stand around the area to get the balls back quickly to those at the cones. The drill starts with each player firing a shot at goal in strict rotation; the goalkeeper moves quickly from goal to goal to re-position himself for each shot. The coach should signal to players when they should shoot so that the goalkeeper is kept working hard to save shots. A reasonable time period for the goalkeeper is about 30–60 seconds, which the coach should monitor since the work is very strenuous.

Development

⚽ Create a competition among the goalkeepers to see who can lose the least number of goals in given time periods.

⚽ Some of the players shooting the ball can be asked to play a certain type of shot, to give the goalkeeper practice in that situation, e.g. a player may attempt to chip the ball over the goalkeeper's head.

⚽ The coach can increase the tempo of the practice whereby each player shoots just as the goalkeeper recovers from the last shot, thus putting him under greater pressure.

PRESSURE DRILL

Purpose

To develop quick reaction, positional sense and to practise handling and agility.

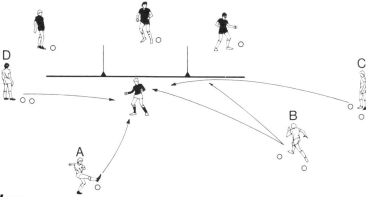

Procedure

A goalkeeper stands in goal, made up with posts, and faces varied serves from A, B, C and D in quick succession, for a set time period, as follows:

A: who stands approximately 10yds away, kicks a hard ball directly to the goalkeeper at chest level

B: stands approximately 15yds away at an angle and drives a hard low shot for the near or far post region

C: stands about 40yds away in a flank position and crosses a high ball in front of the goal

D: who is positioned near the goal line and approximately 15yds away from the goal, hits the ball across the face of the goal.

The goalkeeper defends each service: if he saves the ball by catching it he returns it to the server, if not, the three retrievers get the ball and keep the practice continuous.

Development

⚽ Count the number of successful saves made by each goalkeeper during a given time period.

⚽ The coach can direct the servers to quicken up the service, thus creating more pressure for the goalkeeper.

⚽ Add an attacker who 'listens' near goal, generally challenges the goalkeeper and tries to score from anything that the goalkeeper fails to save.

TURNABOUT GAME

Purpose

To develop positional sense and to practise shot stopping.

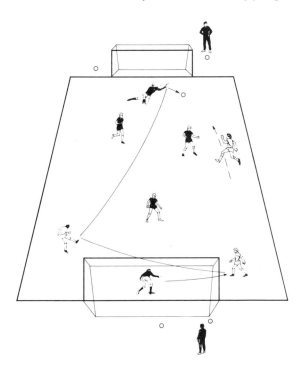

Procedure

In an area approximately 30 x 20yds, two portable goals, defended by goalkeepers, are placed on the end lines. Each goalkeeper has two attackers and one defender stationed near his goal. The game starts with a goalkeeper rolling the ball quickly to one of the unmarked players, who is allowed two touches to either shoot at goal or pass for his colleague to shoot. As soon as the shot is hit the advance player nearer goal looks for a 'knock-down' from the goalkeeper and tries to score. As soon as the shot is dealt with, the goalkeeper then quickly rolls this ball out to set play going in the other direction, thereby maintaining the game's continuity. Use a few retrievers.

Development

⚽ Which goalkeeper loses fewer goals in a given time period?

⚽ Add more players, thus creating more congestion for the goalkeepers.

HIT THE TARGET GAME

Purpose

To practise good all-round distribution of the ball.

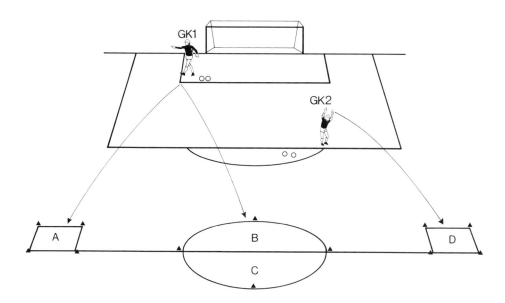

Procedure

Target areas are marked on realistic parts of the field; the goalkeepers, who should have a good supply of balls, in turn distribute the balls and try to hit the target areas where retrievers are positioned. The coach can award scores according to the degree of difficulty in hitting the different target areas, and the goalkeepers can perform under and overarm throws, goal-kicks, and volleys and half-volleys from the hands.

Development

⚽ The coach can introduce an opponent to stand immediately in front of the goalkeeper to see that he complies with the four-step rule before distributing the ball.

⚽ Players can be introduced to stand in front of the target areas and try to intercept throw-outs and kicks from the goalkeeper.

⚽ Record which goalkeeper scores the most successful throws or kicks in a given time period.

WALL REBOUND GAME

Purpose

To develop agility, handling and quick reaction.

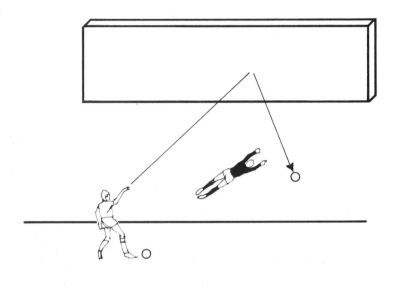

Procedure

The goalkeepers face a wall; lines are marked on the ground at various distances agreed by them. Generally, the nearer the wall the goalkeepers are, the more quick reflexes will be needed and shot stopping practised; if they use the lines which are further from goal, then they are more likely to work on distribution. The goalkeepers throw or kick the ball at the various targets marked on the wall, scoring points if they hit them. Later, one of the goalkeepers stands a few yards away from, and facing, the wall while the other goalkeeper, who is positioned behind him, throws or kicks the ball so that it rebounds from the wall. The goalkeeper nearer the wall is not allowed to watch the service, but dives to save the ball as it rebounds.

Development

⚽ Quicken the speed of the service.

⚽ Add another server so that the ball is served alternately from both sides.

⚽ Determine which goalkeeper makes the most saves in a set time period.

DIVING SEQUENCE DRILL

Purpose

To develop good diving technique.

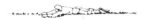

Procedure

A portable goal is set up in a soft diving area; the goalkeeper positions himself in the centre of his goal a few yards in advance of his goal line, with the coach facing him several yards away. The coach serves him a set number of balls (6–12) or, better still, goalkeepers work in pairs and one defends while the other serves (they should change over after a set period). The server should deliver a certain type of ball in a set routine as follows:

(1) a slow rolling ball
(2) a bouncing or medium-height ball
(3) a slow high ball.

The goalkeeper should be stretched gradually by serving the ball further away each time (remember to serve the ball to *both* sides of the goalkeeper). He should also be made to use a set sequence of defence techniques, which progressively gets more difficult, e.g.:

⚽ laying on his side   ⚽ squatting down on his heels

⚽ sitting to face the ball   ⚽ diving over a ball or crouching player

⚽ on one/both knees   ⚽ assuming a basic crouching position.

Development

⚽ The coach can stage a competition between the goalkeepers, with a set number of serves each or a set time limit.

⚽ The coach can introduce an opponent to stand near the goal and score if the goalkeeper fails to save the ball correctly.

DEFLECTION DRILL

Purpose

To practise diving full length to deflect goal-bound shots around the posts.

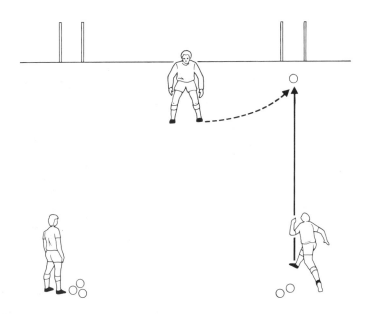

Procedure

Two small goals about 1 yd wide are set up with poles or markers about 10 yds apart. Two players with a supply of three balls each stand directly in front of the targets about 10 yds away. The goalkeeper stands in the centre between the goals. The first server strikes the ball at a medium pace, trying to play it through the target as the goalkeeper moves across quickly in an effort to tip it with an outstretched hand around the post. As soon as he does this, the other server passes the ball into the other goal for the goalkeeper to recover and try to deflect the ball. He should have six continuous services to deal with. The servers need to time and judge their passes so that the goalkeeper can save the shot with difficulty.

Development

⚽ Move the goals further apart so that the goalkeeper needs to cover more ground to make his saves.

⚽ Vary the service a little to make things more realistic and difficult for the goalkeeper, e.g. bouncing or slow looping shots on occasion.

SECTION 2
Fitness Practices

Zvonimir Boban, the Croatian international, has all the necessary qualities of the modern midfielder, including technical proficiency, a sound tactical 'brain', a good mental attitude to competitive situations, and the lung power which enables him to run effectively non-stop for 90 minutes.

Although soccer training has progressed from merely concentrating on practising the skills to be employed within the game, many coaches are still only paying lip-service to the importance of fitness. Many of the so-called 'fitness' schedules are boring, do not have the effect that the coaches claim they will have, and are not designed to ensure *improved* speed, strength and endurance, etc.

The following pages contain well-tried activities which are easily organised, and which aim to provide enjoyable variety while ensuring improved fitness.

The 'doubting Thomases' will claim that activities without a ball are not very relevant. But if one considers that running with a ball at your feet slows you down, then it is obvious that you cannot improve speed by running like this, nor can endurance be increased by running at a slow pace regularly! Anyway, most players in a soccer game are running *without* the ball for *most* of the time.

What is needed is for the coach to create an intelligent mix of skills practices, running, gymnasium work and games to ensure the all-round soccer improvement of his team.

In addition to the games and drills from Section 1 (in which the emphasis was on improving skill and tactics), a soccer coach needs to present modified games or other forms of activity that cater for improving:

⚽ *running endurance* (Increasing the player's ability to run almost non-stop at different speeds throughout the game.)

⚽ *muscular endurance* (Improving a player's ability to jump, head, trap, dribble, tackle, kick, pass, screen, twist, turn and change direction constantly, with some energy still in reserve afterwards, for at least 90 minutes of an arduous game.)

⚽ *strength* (Enabling a player to outjump, kick further, kick harder, tackle harder, throw further, look better and feel better than others, and to avoid injury.)

⚽ *speed* (Gaining the magic 'extra yard' of speed with or without the ball; improving agility and reaction time.)

The above four qualities may be acquired by using practices such as those described in the following pages.

RUNNING ENDURANCE

Pre-season

Not all soccer players will rest completely during their 'off-season', but neither will the majority keep in regular training! It is imperative, therefore, when returning to start the official club training, that a foundation of heart/lung work be introduced *gradually* before the really energetic work begins. How often it is that a season commences with one or two players in a club having been injured during pre-season training!

The best form of basic training is that covering distances of from 2 to 3 miles, or 3000 to 5000 metres on grass, mixing the speed from walking, to jogging and striding out. On such occasions the coach should accompany the players to ensure that they are gaining maximum benefit, or alternatively use an athlete who has the capacity to stay with the squad over longish distances.

Fartlek

This is an activity which naturally develops from the pre-season building-up runs.

In this form of activity, the coach works out a short cross-country distance and route in his mind, gets his players assembled and sets off at a jogging pace. After about 800 metres he will stop, and all players will be required to do some exercises, such as press-ups, squat jumps or even pulling and pushing games. Then the squad will set off jogging again.

The coach may now set a target, e.g. tree, building, lamp-post, etc., about 100 metres ahead to which all players will be urged to sprint (a penalty of five press-ups may be 'paid' by the last player there). After this, all can walk 100 metres, jog 100 metres, and then sprint 100 metres, etc.

Occasional stops can be made to get the breath steady and also to give players more exercises to perform. The emphasis must be on mixing the speeds (as happens in a game) and ensuring the players are put in a happy frame of mind with enjoyable competition and amusing asides.

Indian file run

Those with limited facilities and only a soccer field to train on can still organise enjoyable running programmes that gradually progress from gentle running to full-out sprinting.

Included in this classification is the Indian file run which can consist of one long line of players jogging around a soccer field. When the coach blows the whistle the last player runs to become the first in the 'Indian file'. If the group is divided into two or more 'files', then the coach may ask the last one in each file to try to get to the front of his file before the other. Thus there is a mixture of fast and slow running which is of benefit to all players.

Continuous relay

Here the group of players is divided into a number of teams of perhaps seven, eight or nine players. The various players are positioned around the pitch as illustrated in the diagram below.

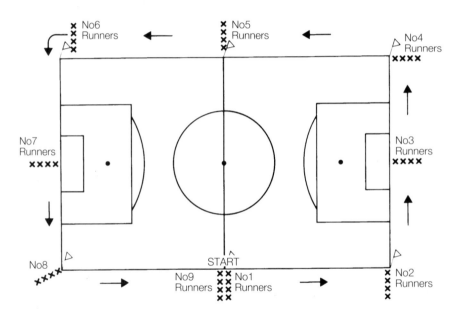

It is imperative that at the start there are *two* players from each team, one being the first runner, the other the last in the team. On the whistle being blown by the coach, no.1 runner in each team runs and passes a piece of wood or relay baton to his no.2. The no.2 then runs to pass the baton to no.3, etc. After handing over the baton each player *must* stop running and wait at the hand-over point until the next time the baton is brought round. Thus the race could continue until all players have progressed around the field and back to their starting positions – a total of about eight fast sprints (the baton goes around the track eight times) with a rest between. The race can be repeated after a short break.

Alternatively, a definite period of, say, ten or more minutes can be set. The whistle is blown at the end of the allotted time, and the team leading is declared the winner.

Individual races

Occasionally races can be introduced to check whether players are improving in endurance; to provide valuable exercise when the fields are covered with snow and soccer cannot be played on them; to check on players' recovery after injury; and to provide enjoyment!

The races need only be over about 2 miles (3000 metres); each player must be properly timed and recorded thus:

Name	Time (mins/secs)	Time from runner in front (secs)	Time from last runner (mins/secs)
Williams	9.30	0	1.10
Jones	9.40	10	1.0
Davies	9.55	15	0.45
Evans	10.0	5	0.40
Griffiths	10.20	20	0.20
Lloyd	10.25	5	0.15
Thomas	10.30	5	0.10
Matthias	10.40	10	0.0

This can be placed on a notice board so that a number of targets can be set for future races, i.e. the coach can set each player a target either to:

⚽ win

⚽ or beat a player who beat him previously

⚽ or beat his own previous time

⚽ or close the time difference between the player ahead of him last time

⚽ or increase the time difference between the player behind him last time.

The coach could also use this form of running in another way, by setting off Matthias first, Thomas 10 seconds later, Lloyd another 5 seconds later and then Griffiths another 20 seconds later, etc. (*see* the last column in the table above). With this scheme, theoretically, all should dead-heat at the finish! The objective for each is to overtake the player ahead, and/or to beat his previous time for the course.

Yet another method is to pair bad and good players together, e.g.:

⚽ Williams would partner Matthias

⚽ Jones would partner Thomas

⚽ Davies would partner Lloyd

⚽ Evans would partner Griffiths.

In this race the total of the pairs would count. Thus the better player should help along the other, except towards the end when he will cover the last 800 metres fast to cut down the aggregate time.

The important thing about distance running is that it is presented in an interesting fashion and not as a punishment!

From time to time races can be run in the opposite direction – the essence of good training planning is *variety*.

Paarlauf

Once a good basis of training has been covered, more demanding practices can be introduced to maintain heart and lung endurance.

Players can be divided into pairs. An eight-lap (or other distance) race is proposed, which the two players share. They can either run alternate laps (a slow method) or a half-lap each as illustrated below; in the latter case each player will have to run across the field after handing over the baton in order to receive it from his partner at the half-lap point.

This is arduous *but beneficial*; it should be used only as an occasional exercise, not daily!

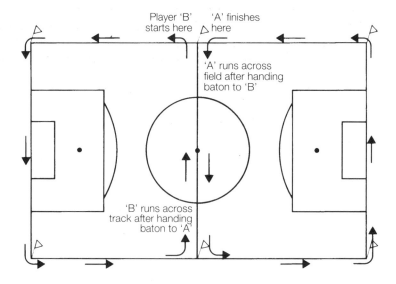

Resistance running

This form of running is extremely hard work, but concentrates a great deal of effort into a seemingly short period of time.

It includes running up steep hills. Whether the hills are of sand, coal, snow or mud does not matter as long as they are from 50 to 100 metres long; the players should use their arms very vigorously. The number of times players have to sprint up these hills and walk back down will be gauged by the coach. He should ignore any complaints on the grounds that if it is an uncomfortable activity it could be doing the players some good!

Other forms of resistance running include the use of belts or harnesses, which are designed to ensure they inflict no injury on the players. They may be old car inner tubes, specially made harnesses and gymnastics belts, but *not* skipping ropes! The players first pair off and then the one at the back applies resistance so that the front runner has to drive hard with his legs and arms in order to run the 40 metres or so. On reaching that point they exchange places for the return journey. A total of about ten runs in the harness can be gradually built up over a period of weeks.

Other resistance work, such as running in boots or with weighted belts, etc., can be introduced by the coach as a contribution to variety if he needs it, especially in prolonged periods of absence from fields owing to bad weather conditions.

Pursuit plan

In this practice a number of teams, e.g. eight or ten, each consisting of four players, sit near a flag positioned as on the diagram below. On the command 'Go' or whistle start, the players cover the pattern movement indicated as fast as they can, but at the same time they must try to keep together to encourage the slower team members. The first team to sit down again in its original position is the winner.

It looks simple, but as shown in the diagram every player covers over 700 metres (nearly half a mile) at a very fast pace.

(Each group of four could consist of a defender, striker, goalkeeper, midfield player, etc.)

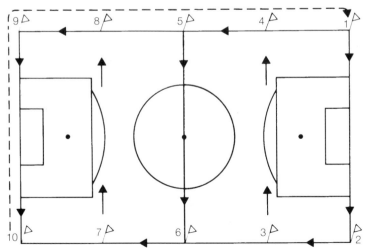

MUSCLE ENDURANCE

Circuit training

This activity is a *must* for soccer players and has many advantages.

⚽ It contains a variety of different exercises that work all major muscle groups.

⚽ It is easily organised, even in a confined space.

It need only be done for up to 30 minutes each week.

⚽ Players work at their own rate on a 'tailor-made' schedule.

⚽ It can be adapted for indoor or outdoor use.

⚽ It is an excellent motivator because coaches and players can see fitness improvement and progress.

⚽ It can be used as an *accurate* test to find out whether a player is fully recovered from an injury.

The gymnasium, hall, social club bar area, or outdoor space can be drawn on a diagram so that all players can be shown where each exercise takes place.

On the first occasion a quick demonstration of each exercise will be needed from the coach; players will be paired off so that while no.1 is exercising, no.2 counts the number of times his partner performs the exercises in 60 seconds and records them on a card. Then no.2 exercises while no.1 counts, so that the testing is over 60 seconds with each player getting about 3 minutes' rest before he does the next exercise, i.e. the coach will blow his whistle at 1-minute intervals and ensure that the following procedure is adopted:

⚽ **6.00–6.01pm**
No.1 player exercises, no.2 player counts no.1's score.

⚽ **6.01–6.02pm**
No.2 makes a note of no.1's score on no.1's card, then no.2 gets ready to start.

⚽ **6.02–6.03pm**
No.2 exercises, no.1 counts no.2's score.

⚽ **6.03–6.04pm**
No.1 makes a note of no.2's score on no.2's card, then no.1 gets ready for the next exercise.

⚽ **6.04–6.05pm**
No.1 attempts the next exercise, no.2 counts the score.

The exercises should be laid out in such a way that an arm exercise is followed by an abdominal exercise and then a leg exercise, etc. The layout below is for use in a gymnasium; the coach can alter it according to the facilities and equipment he has available. The number of exercises should normally be eight to ten.

On the first occasion, tests will be made as described; each player is given his own postcard which will record his test scores and which will be kept by the coach after each session. Cards can be marked as follows.

CIRCUIT								
NAME *FRED SMITH*		POSITION *GOALKEEPER*						
HEIGHT *1·81M*		WEIGHT *85 kg.*						
DATE	1	2	3	4	5	6	7	8
TEST *1·8·94*	30	61	27	52	47	59	18	8
3 x CIRCUIT *8·8·94*	15	31	14	26	24	25	9	4
RETEST *12·9·94*	33	64	30	54	50	63	19	9
3 x CIRCUIT *19·9·94*	17	32	15	27	25	32	10	4

Reverse side

WEEK BEGINNING	TIME TAKEN		NOTES
	MINUTES	SECONDS	
8·8·94	24	49	
15·8·94	23	17	
22·8·94	23	08	
29·8·94	21	23	
5·9·94	18	14	RETEST NEXT WEEK
19·9·94	25	13	
26·9·94	23	42	

Immediately the player has been tested, his score on each test is recorded on his circuit card. On the line below (preferably in a different coloured ink) half of each of the scores is written.

The following week, on the occasion of the player's first circuit training session, he is required to perform the half scores during his first circuit of the gymnasium, then continue with a second circuit of the half scores, and finally a third circuit of the gymnasium performing the half scores. That is, he completes *three* circuits of the gymnasium, performing *half* of his maximum test scores each time. He is thus spreading the load over a long period – the basis of endurance work.

By recording the total time he takes to do the three circuits each week, he will detect a rapid improvement. Once the coach notices that the total time taken is below 20 minutes, he will re-test the player for maximum effort on each exercise, and require him to continue with 3 x half maximum score circuits.

Occasionally, as a relief from the circuit card system, the coach will pair players of approximately equal fitness ability. While no.1 aims for maximum over 1 minute at each of the eight exercises, no.2 counts and checks for cheating; then no.2 tries to beat no.1's score in a series, such as:

⚽ no.1 attempts exercise 1 for 60 seconds; no.2 counts; 30 seconds rest

⚽ no.2 attempts to beat no.1's score on exercise 1; 30 seconds rest

⚽ no.1 attempts exercise 2 for 60 seconds; no.2 counts; 30 seconds rest

⚽ no.2 attempts to beat no.1's score on exercise 2, etc.

Some coaches might prefer to devise a specific soccer circuit including ball skill activities. Sometimes these are merely distractions from what a soccer player needs, i.e. hard, continuous activity in which he has to withstand a great deal of pain. The coach will know his players' abilities and industriousness, and he should remind them that there is no substitute for hard work. If players wish to reach the top, they will need to endure discomfort regularly in training.

STRENGTH WORK

One of the main reasons why soccer players and their trainers have avoided weight training over the years has been the risk of injury to the players. Other contributing factors have included trainers' ignorance of what strength really is; the fear of players becoming 'muscle-bound' or putting on weight; cost of equipment, or shortage of space; and obsession with the need to relate exercise to the soccer field and working with a ball.

Leading trainers now accept, however, that weight training is a necessity for the development of strength, and that soccer players need to weight train. Fortunately, in recent years safer methods of strength training have been devised to eliminate the risk of injury.

'Contigyms' and other multi-station machines

The 'new' machinery, which coaches now seem happy to use, permits large groups of people to work in a confined space. It prevents injuries caused by players dropping weights on themselves or others, and it also prevents injuries from incorrect lifting and handling of weight. An individual can train safely on the equipment without the aid of a partner to help with the weight; this is ideal for soccer players rehabilitating after injury.

With the new machinery, it is important to remember that a player's *strength* is only increased when his muscles are made to cope with extra *weights*, and *not* a large number of repetitions, i.e. to increase strength, a soccer player needs to deal with *fewer repetitions* and *more weight* than he would use in endurance work.

Endurance work, on the other hand, consists of exercises which are performed with many repetitions, and a light-weight strength programme should be followed, e.g. a series of six lifts followed by a minute massaging the muscle groups exercised; then another six lifts, a minute massage, and finally another six lifts. In other words, this involves three sets of six repetitions, or '3 x 6'. The weight used will depend on the size of the player and his strength. But it is imperative that if he can cope easily with, for example 3 x 6 with 80 lbs (35 kg), then he should add another 5 lbs (2 kg) the next session, so that the strength sessions continually extend him.

Occasionally a 'pyramid' system can be introduced for variety, i.e. the player starts with a heavy weight, e.g. 100 lbs (40 kg), and lifts it once; he reduces the weight to 90 lbs (35 kg) and lifts it twice; he reduces the weight to 80 lbs (30 kg) and lifts it three times; he then reduces the weight to 70 lbs (25 kg) and lifts it four times; finally, he reduces the weight to 60 lbs (20 kg) and lifts it five times.

Arm strength

A number of exercises are appropriate, including:

⚽ bench press

⚽ seated press

⚽ lateral behind neck.

Bench press (multigym) The player lies on the bench, feet flat on the floor, holding the bar perpendicularly over the chest. The bar is pressed firmly into the air and lowered slowly in the following sequence: 1 x lowest weight; 2 x next weight up; 3 x further weight up, etc. until fatigue sets in. This is called a 'pyramid' system.

Seated press In this exercise, the weight is pressed high and quickly into the air, but lowered slowly while sitting. The pyramid system could be used, or a low weight selected and raised six times; follow this with a 30 second rest; then raise the weight another six times; then another 30 second rest; then raise the bar a final six times.

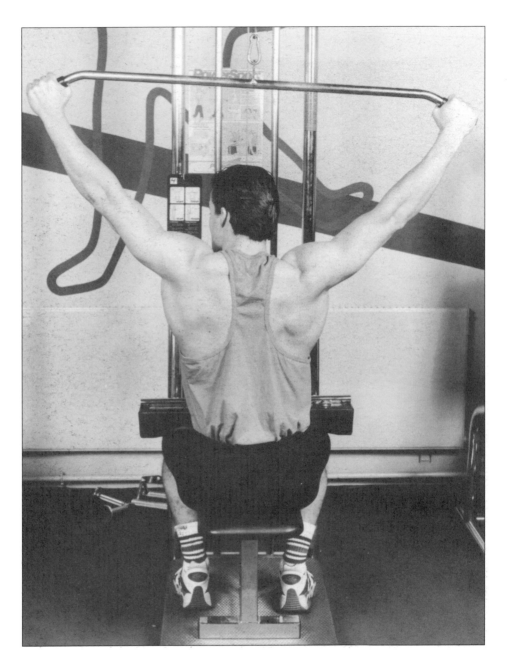

Lateral behind neck *(above and right) Sitting or kneeling, the bar is set for a 3 x 6 system as with the seated press exercise. The bar is pulled down strongly to the shoulders behind the neck, then it is released slowly upwards. Breathing in most exercises should be through the mouth – out during the exertion and in during the relaxing phase.*

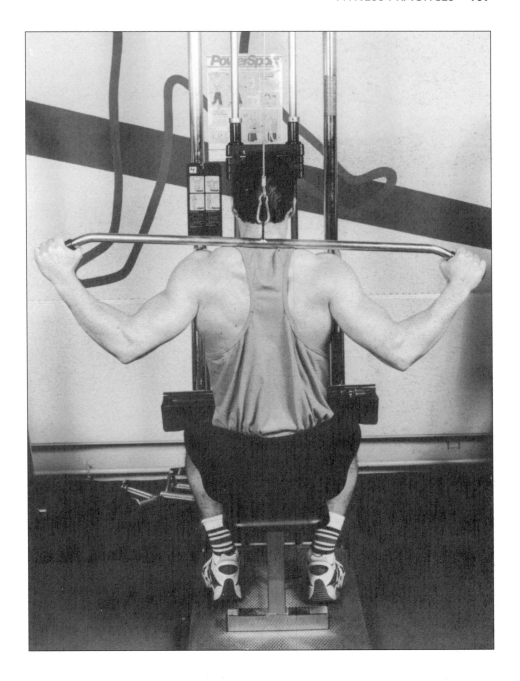

Leg strength

Appropriate exercises include:

⚽ leg press ⚽ leg extension ⚽ half squat ⚽ leg flexion.

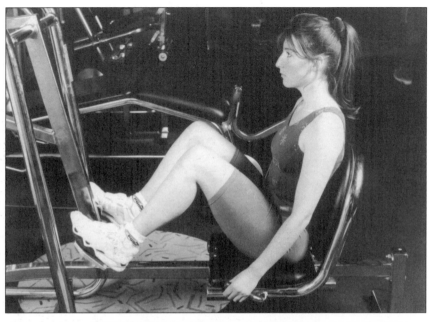

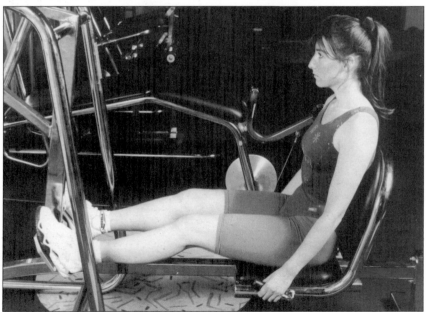

Leg press *(left) Set the weight for a 3 x 6 system. The player is seated, hands grasping the handles. The feet are ready to exert pressure on the footrests. The seat must be set to ensure that the knees are at an angle of 90° to the floor – this will prevent injury. The weight is pushed hard towards a straight leg position, then slowly bent to the 90° position.*

Leg extension *(right) Use a 3 x 6 system. The feet are placed under the pads. Gripping the seat or the handles, and with the back upright, the legs are raised to a straight position. They are then slowly lowered and further repetitions are made.*

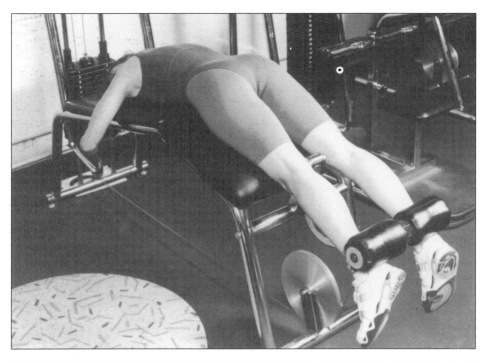

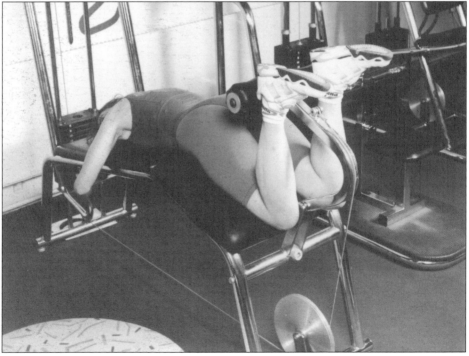

Leg flexion (left) The back of the legs are very much neglected. The player raises the weight by pulling on the pads with the back of the heels. The action is towards the buttocks. Then the weight is lowered until the legs are straight again. Using 3 x 6 repetitions, a short rest is taken between each group of six.

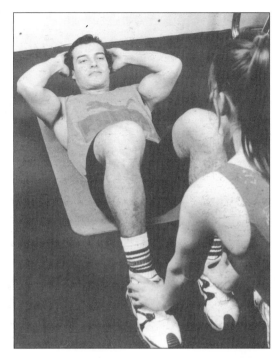

Trunk strength

Appropriate exercises include:

⚽ abdominal curl

⚽ seated rowing.

Abdominal curl (right) The feet are held down by a partner or held under a wall bar, etc. A small weight (5 kg) can be held behind the head, but beginners must start with no weight at all. The body is raised so that the elbows touch the knees. Then the body is lowered fully to the floor again. Adopt a 3 x 6 system.

Barbells and dumb-bells

Those soccer clubs that cannot afford the new strength machinery need not despair. The 'old ironmongery' is still of immense value; in fact, in some sports, such as athletics, bars, weights and collars are preferred.

It is important to emphasise that all safety precautions must be taken; players must be taught how to lift properly; heavy weights must be introduced gradually after a good 'grounding' using lighter weights; players should never train alone using this method.

Arm strength
Appropriate exercises include:

⚽ dumb-bell punch   ⚽ bent arm pullover

⚽ military press   ⚽ lateral raise.

⚽ bench press

Military press (above) The feet are shoulder width apart, with the toes pointing forwards. The bar is on the floor with the player's feet underneath. With the head up and the back straight, the bar is lifted vigorously to the player's chest. It is pushed up above the head vigorously and lowered to the chest slowly six times, then lowered to the floor. After 30 seconds rest, make six further presses; another 30 seconds rest; a further six presses. This exercise requires supervision initially.

Dumb-bell punch (left) The feet are shoulder width apart, with the toes pointing forwards. The dumb-bells are punched into the air with alternate arms and lowered to the shoulder. The 3 x 6 system can be used, with progressively heavier weights being introduced.

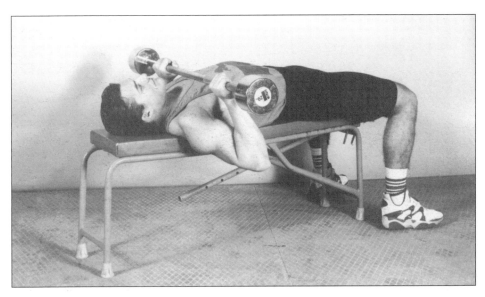

Bench press (barbell) *Lying on a bench and with the feet on the floor, the player is normally passed the bar by a colleague. The bar is pushed up vigorously and then lowered slowly to the chest. A 3 x 6 system is recommended, with three players working together to ensure that the lifter does not get injured.*

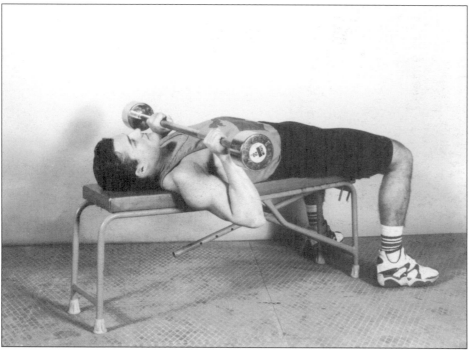

Bent arm pullover *Lying on the bench with the feet flat on the floor, the player raises the bar from behind him to a vertical position. It is then lowered to the chest before it is returned to the floor behind. (Stiff-shouldered players should lower the bar as far as they can!) A 3 x 6 system is appropriate.*

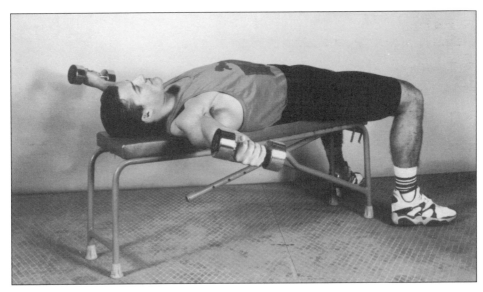

Lateral raise Lying on the bench, the player holds the dumb-bells with arms outstretched. They are then lifted outwards and high until they meet above the chest, before they are lowered again. A 3 x 6 system is appropriate.

Leg strength
Appropriate exercises include:

⚽ half squat

⚽ step on bench

⚽ heel raise.

Half squat The player's heels should be off the floor on a 1-inch block of wood, or a pair of built-up shoes could be used. The player is helped by two colleagues, who lift the bar on to his shoulders behind the neck. With the knees bending forwards and the toes pointing forwards, the player lowers the body until reaching a 90° position at the knees in relation to the floor. The head is held up, and the legs are then straightened to the starting position. Adopt a 3 x 6 system.

Step on bench Use approximately the same weight as in the half squat. The player steps on and off a bench, slowly and with great care. Alternate the legs that step on and off. Close supervision is a must for this exercise. A 3 x 6 system is recommended.

Heel raise *Use approximately the same weight as in the half squat exercise. The player raises his body up on to his toes, with the barbell firmly held on the shoulders. The 'up' position should be held for ten seconds, then the heels are lowered to the floor. A 3 x 6 system is appropriate.*

Trunk strength

Appropriate exercises include:

⚽ dead lift

⚽ inclined trunk twists.

Dead lift *The player's feet are under the bar, with the back straight and the eyes and head up. Pulling with the arms and pushing with the legs, the weight is lifted to thigh height. After a few seconds it is lowered again, and the exercise is repeated in a 3 x 6 system.*

Other methods

In addition to the equipment described previously, there is a plethora of pulleys, medicine balls, rowing machines, bicycles, chest expanders and dynamometers for which there is a 'strengthening effect' claim.

A wise coach will be able to discern the relative merits of these well-advertised types of apparatus. But he and his players cannot escape the fact that strength is only gained through very hard work. This work should be carefully controlled and the effort applied measurable; the amount can then be gradually increased as each player's strength develops.

The coach whose team cannot afford much extra equipment can resort to vigorous partner activities, such as wheelbarrow races, leap frog, hopping over hurdles, etc. to supplement the training. With a little ingenuity he and his players will be able to provide substitute 'weights' made out of old scrap metal, concrete and long poles. 'Where there is a will, there's a way!'

GAINING SPEED

There are numerous reasons why a soccer player may not be as fast as he, or his coach, would wish, such as:

- he is too heavy
- his legs are not strong enough to propel his body very far on each stride he takes
- he does not practise sprinting often enough.

The cure for the first problem is easy, and it is assured by all good coaches who regularly check the weight of their players. A good strength programme, such as that outlined earlier, will overcome the second difficulty. The third problem is not always immediately recognised by coaches or players. Often they will readily accept the need to practise shooting at goal, dribbling, heading and controlling the ball, but assume that increased speed is acquired incidentally.

Sprinting is a *fundamental skill* that soccer players need to practise in order to improve their speed. (In the following practises spiked shoes are unnecessary. Studded soccer boots used for running on grass, as in the game, would be appropriate.)

Repetition running

A soccer squad is divided into groups of four along the goal line; these four players should be of approximately equal sprinting ability. They then run at 'flat-out' speed to the half-way line and walk back; this is repeated a number of times.

A good session would proceed as follows: six sprints (walking back after each) followed by 3 minutes or so rest; then two more sets of sprinting and resting; and finally another six sprints. This is usually referred to as four sets of six repetitions of 50 metres, or 4 x 6 x 50 m.

Those who complain about doing such an arduous workout will be those who dislike hard work. A common excuse is that a player rarely has to run 50 metres in a game. The answer to this criticism is that by improving a player's speed over 50 metres, his speed over 20 metres is also increased *and* it enables him to run *many more* fast 25-metre runs within the game without becoming tired.

Up and down the clock

To relieve the possible boredom in repetition running the work can occasionally be presented in a different fashion: grouped in fours on the goal line, the players sprint to cones laid out at various intervals. Thus they sprint 20 metres; walk back to the starting line; sprint 30 metres; walk back; sprint 40 metres; walk back; sprint 50 metres; walk back; sprint 60 metres; walk back; sprint 70 metres. After about 3 minutes rest, they then sprint 70 metres; walk back; sprint 60 metres; walk back; sprint 50 metres; walk back; sprint 40 metres; walk back; sprint 30 metres; walk back; sprint 20 metres.

After a further 3 minutes rest, they then sprint 'up the clock', i.e. 20 metres; 30 metres; 40 metres; 50 metres; 60 metres; 70 metres.

After another 3 minutes rest, they sprint 'down the clock', i.e. a descending distance: 70 metres; 60 metres; 50 metres; 40 metres; 30 metres; 20 metres.

During all speed practices, the coach must urge the players to further effort. Merely covering the distances will not improve speed unless they are putting in a great deal of effort.

Arm and leg drive

Many games players (and athletes!) do not realise the importance of the arms in increasing speed. Some soccer players develop massive legs, but do little work on arm strength and development.

A useful practice to illustrate the value of the arms is to make soccer players run a half-field distance twice, the first time with their hands

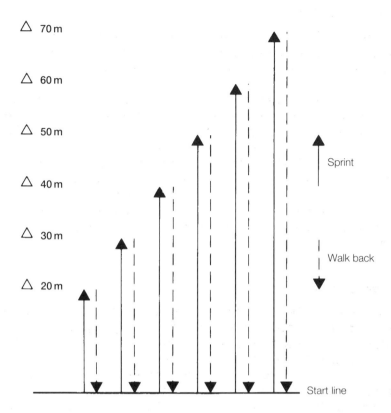

clasped behind their backs, and the second time with their arms moving vigorously; the difference will astound them.

A good way to increase speed over a few metres is to get players lined up on the goal line and have a competition to see who can reach the 18-yd line in the fewest number of strides. The vigorous use of the arms, and the driving of the feet right to the end of the toes, will help give the player a feeling of the power he should generate when moving for a ball a few yards away.

Shuttle relays

To prevent cheating it is necessary to introduce a relay baton, or piece of wood. Team races usually result in extra effort being put into the event, thus improving each player's speed.

As many teams as desired are chosen and lined up as illustrated on page 124. When the coach blows his whistle, the no.1 in each team sprints from the half-way line towards the no.2, who must receive the baton *behind* the goal line and sprint to pass the baton to no.3, and so on.

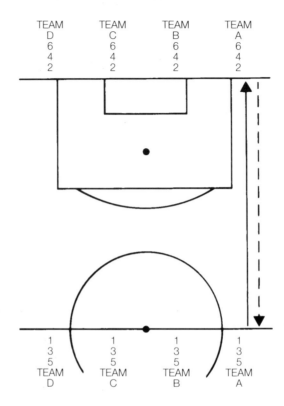

Teams should be kept to small numbers, such as six players, to prevent boredom in standing still for long periods. The relay races could be ten in number, with only one or two minutes rest between. The team that wins the most first places out of the ten races is the winner.

Potato race

Combining short bursts of speed with changes of direction, this activity is easily organised. A number of potatoes, or training bibs, relay batons, bean bags, old tennis balls, quoits, or similar objects, are needed. They are placed *in twos* (one from each pair acts as a marker), 5 metres apart, as illustrated on the next page. Teams line up facing their potatoes, and on the command 'Go', the first player in each line runs to collect one potato and returns to the start as before, and so on. When no.1 has collected all five potatoes, one at a time, no.2 then runs to put them back, one at a time, next to the remaining marker potatoes.

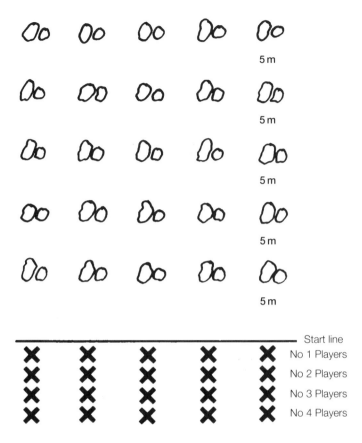

The team to finish replacing all the potatoes after all the players have run obviously wins. The practice can, of course, be repeated a number of times, but it is hard work, so the coach should not expect the players to run this 150 metres of sprinting and turning many times. The potato race is a useful practice with which to start or finish a training session.

Use of the ball

Some coaches insist that players always have a ball at their feet during training sessions. Although practice with the ball is imperative, running with the ball for much of the time does slow players down. To increase the speed of the players, therefore, several sessions *without* the ball are absolutely essential.

INDEX